Python for OSINT

Tracking and Profiling Targets

Jason Bourny

1

3

Disclaimer

The information provided in "**Python for OSINT: Tracking and Profiling Targets**" by **Jason Bourny** is intended solely for educational and informational purposes. This book is designed to enhance your understanding of advanced web scraping and data extraction methods using Python in the context of open-source intelligence (OSINT).

Readers are advised to seek the guidance of qualified professionals before applying any techniques described herein to real-world scenarios. The author and publisher of this book are not responsible for any actions taken based on the information provided, nor for any consequences arising from such actions.

Other books in the Python for Hackers series

"Python for Wireless Hacking: Exploiting Wi-Fi Networks and Bluetooth Devices"

"Advanced Python Scripting for Kali Linux: Exploiting Security Weaknesses"

"Python for Cryptography and Steganography: Concealing and Revealing Secrets"

"Python for Web Hackers: Mastering Black Hat Techniques"

" Python IoT Infiltration: Hacking Internet of Things Devices"

" Python for Smartphone Hacking: Mobile Intrusions"

"Python for Browser Hackers: Attack and Exploit Vulnerabilities on the Web"

"Infernal Python Botnets Hackers: Building and Controlling Networks of Infected Devices"

Introduction

Welcome to **"Python for OSINT: Tracking and Profiling Targets,"** your gateway to mastering the art and science of advanced web scraping and data extraction. In an era where information is the new gold, the ability to mine data efficiently and effectively can set you apart as a formidable force in the world of hacking, penetration testing, and open-source intelligence (OSINT).

This is crafted specifically for professionals and enthusiasts like you who are driven by a relentless pursuit of knowledge and the power that comes with it. Whether you're a seasoned hacker looking to sharpen your skills or a penetration tester aiming to elevate your game, this comprehensive guide is your roadmap to uncovering the hidden corners of the web.

Imagine having the capability to effortlessly extract valuable data from even the most obscure websites, turning the internet into your personal treasure trove. With Python as your tool of choice, you'll learn to navigate the complexities of web protocols, bypass security measures, and gather intelligence with precision and stealth. This isn't just about scraping data; it's about transforming raw information into actionable insights.

In the pages that follow, you'll dive deep into sophisticated techniques that go beyond the basics. We'll cover everything from setting up your Python environment for optimal performance to leveraging powerful libraries like BeautifulSoup, Scrapy, and Selenium. You'll explore real-world scenarios where these skills are applied to track targets, profile individuals, and map out networks with unparalleled accuracy.

Each chapter is designed to build your expertise step-by-step, ensuring that you not only understand the theory but also gain hands-on experience through practical examples and exercises. You'll discover how to automate data collection, parse complex datasets, and employ machine learning algorithms to predict and analyze trends.

By the end of this book, you'll be equipped with a toolkit of advanced methods that will enhance your OSINT capabilities and give you a significant edge in your endeavors. You'll be ready to tackle the most challenging data extraction tasks, armed with knowledge that is both cutting-edge and highly practical.

So, are you ready to unlock the full potential of Python for OSINT? Dive in and transform the way you approach data extraction and web scraping. The world of hidden data is vast, and your journey to mastering it starts here.

Chapter 1: Python for OSINT

Python is a versatile programming language that is widely used in various fields, including Open Source Intelligence (OSINT). OSINT refers to the collection and analysis of publicly available information to gather intelligence and insights. Python is particularly well-suited for OSINT tasks due to its simplicity, readability, and extensive libraries that can be used to automate data collection, analysis, and visualization.

In this introduction to Python for OSINT, we will explore some of the key concepts and tools that can be used to leverage Python for intelligence gathering and analysis. Whether you are a beginner or an experienced Python programmer, this guide will provide you with the necessary knowledge to get started with using Python for OSINT.

One of the main advantages of using Python for OSINT is its ease of use and readability. Python's syntax is simple and straightforward, making it easy for beginners to learn and understand. Additionally, Python has a large and active community of developers who create and maintain a wide range of libraries that can be used for various tasks, including web scraping, data analysis, and visualization.

When it comes to OSINT, one of the most common tasks is web scraping, which involves extracting data from websites. Python has several libraries, such as BeautifulSoup and Scrapy, that can be used to scrape websites and extract relevant information. These libraries make it easy to automate the process of collecting data from multiple sources, saving time and effort.

Another important aspect of OSINT is data analysis and visualization. Python has libraries such as Pandas and Matplotlib that can be used to analyze and visualize data in a variety of ways. These libraries make it easy to manipulate and explore data, allowing for deeper insights to be gained from the information collected.

In addition to web scraping and data analysis, Python can also be used for tasks such as geospatial analysis, social media monitoring, and sentiment analysis. Python's versatility and extensibility make it a powerful tool for a wide range of OSINT tasks.

To get started with using Python for OSINT, it is important to have a basic understanding of the Python programming language. There are many resources available online, including tutorials, documentation, and forums, that can help you learn Python quickly and efficiently.

Once you have a good grasp of Python basics, you can start exploring some of the libraries and tools that are commonly used in OSINT. For example, you can use BeautifulSoup to scrape websites, Pandas to analyze data, and Matplotlib to visualize your findings.

In conclusion, Python is a powerful and versatile programming language that is well-suited for OSINT tasks. By leveraging Python's simplicity, readability, and extensive libraries, you can automate data collection, analysis, and visualization, making it easier to gather intelligence and insights from publicly available information.

Whether you are a beginner or an experienced Python programmer, learning Python for OSINT can help you become more efficient and effective in your intelligence gathering efforts.

What is OSINT?

OSINT, or Open Source Intelligence, is a term used to describe the collection and analysis of information that is publicly available. This information can be found on the internet, in newspapers, on social media, and in other public sources. OSINT is used by a variety of organizations, including government agencies, law enforcement, and private companies, to gather intelligence on a wide range of topics.

One of the key benefits of OSINT is that it is a cost-effective way to gather information. Unlike traditional intelligence gathering methods, which can be time-consuming and expensive, OSINT relies on publicly available sources that are often free or low-cost. This makes it accessible to a wide range of organizations, regardless of their budget.

OSINT can be used to gather information on a variety of topics, including individuals, organizations, and events. For example, law enforcement agencies may use OSINT to gather information on suspects or criminal organizations, while private companies may use it to gather information on competitors or market trends. OSINT can also be used to monitor social media for potential threats or to gather information on political events or protests.

There are a variety of tools and techniques that can be used to gather OSINT. These include search engines, social media monitoring tools, and data mining software. These tools can be used to gather information from a wide range of sources, including websites, social media platforms, and online forums.

One of the key challenges of OSINT is verifying the accuracy of the information gathered. Because OSINT relies on publicly available sources, there is always a risk that the information may be inaccurate or misleading. This is why it is important for organizations to carefully evaluate the sources of their information and cross-reference it with other sources whenever possible.

Despite these challenges, OSINT can be a valuable tool for organizations looking to gather intelligence on a wide range of topics. By using publicly available sources, organizations can gather information quickly and cost-effectively, allowing them to make informed decisions and stay ahead of potential threats.

In conclusion, OSINT is a valuable tool for organizations looking to gather intelligence on a wide range of topics. By using publicly available sources, organizations can gather information quickly and cost-effectively, allowing them to make informed decisions and stay ahead of potential threats. While there are challenges associated with OSINT, such as verifying the accuracy of information, the benefits of using OSINT far outweigh the risks.

Organizations that are able to effectively use OSINT can gain a competitive advantage and stay ahead of potential threats in an increasingly complex and fast-paced world.

The Power of Python in OSINT

Python has become an indispensable tool in the world of Open Source Intelligence (OSINT) due to its versatility, ease of use, and powerful libraries. OSINT is the practice of collecting and analyzing information from publicly available sources to gather intelligence and insights. Python's flexibility and extensive libraries make it an ideal language for OSINT practitioners to automate tasks, analyze data, and extract valuable information from various sources.

One of the key advantages of using Python in OSINT is its ability to automate repetitive tasks. OSINT professionals often need to gather and analyze large amounts of data from multiple sources, which can be time-consuming and tedious if done manually. Python allows users to write scripts that can automatically retrieve, process, and analyze data from websites, social media platforms, and other sources. This automation not only saves time but also ensures accuracy and consistency in the data collection process.

Python's extensive libraries make it easy for OSINT practitioners to extract and manipulate data from various sources. Libraries such as BeautifulSoup and Scrapy are commonly used to scrape data from websites, while libraries like tweepy and pytwint are used to access and analyze data from social media platforms like Twitter.

These libraries provide pre-built functions and tools that simplify the process of data extraction and analysis, allowing users to focus on interpreting the data rather than writing complex code.

Python's data analysis capabilities are another reason why it is widely used in OSINT. The language has powerful libraries like pandas and numpy that make it easy to clean, process, and analyze large datasets. These libraries allow users to perform tasks such as data cleaning, filtering, aggregation, and visualization with just a few lines of code. This makes it easier for OSINT practitioners to identify patterns, trends, and anomalies in the data, leading to valuable insights and intelligence.

Python's versatility also extends to its ability to interact with APIs and other data sources. Many websites and platforms provide APIs that allow users to access and retrieve data programmatically. Python's requests library makes it easy to interact with APIs and retrieve data in various formats like JSON and XML. This allows OSINT practitioners to access a wide range of data sources, including social media platforms, news websites, and government databases, to gather intelligence and insights.

In addition to its technical capabilities, Python's community and ecosystem also play a significant role in its popularity in the OSINT field. The language has a large and active community of developers, data scientists, and researchers who contribute to open-source projects, share knowledge, and provide support to beginners. This community-driven approach has led to the development of numerous tools, libraries, and resources that cater to the specific needs of OSINT practitioners, making Python an even more attractive choice for professionals in the field.

Overall, the power of Python in OSINT lies in its flexibility, ease of use, powerful libraries, and strong community support. The language's ability to automate tasks, extract and analyze data, interact with APIs, and access a wide range of data sources makes it an indispensable tool for OSINT practitioners looking to gather intelligence and insights from publicly available sources. As the field of OSINT continues to evolve and grow, Python is likely to remain a key tool for professionals seeking to harness the power of data and information in their investigations.

Setting Up Your Python Environment

Python is a powerful and versatile programming language that is widely used in various fields, including web development, data analysis, artificial intelligence, and more. Setting up your Python environment is the first step to start coding in Python. In this article, we will guide you through the process of setting up your Python environment on your computer.

Installing Python:

The first step in setting up your Python environment is to install Python on your computer. You can download the latest version of Python from the official Python website (https://www.python.org/downloads/). Python is available for Windows, macOS, and Linux operating systems.

Once you have downloaded the Python installer, run the installer and follow the on-screen instructions to install Python on your computer. Make sure to check the option to add Python to your system PATH during the installation process, as this will allow you to run Python from the command line.

Installing a Code Editor:

After installing Python, the next step is to choose a code editor for writing and running Python code. There are many code editors available for Python, but some popular choices include Visual Studio Code, PyCharm, and Sublime Text.

You can download and install any of these code editors from their respective websites. Once you have installed a code editor, you can open it and start writing Python code.

Installing Python Packages:

Python comes with a standard library that includes many useful modules and packages. However, you may need to install additional packages for specific tasks. The most common way to install Python packages is to use the pip package manager.

To install a Python package using pip, open a command prompt or terminal window and run the following command:

```
pip install package_name
```

Replace `package_name` with the name of the package you want to install. For example, to install the NumPy package for numerical computing, you can run the following command:

```
pip install numpy
```

Setting up a Virtual Environment:

A virtual environment is a self-contained directory that contains a specific version of Python and its dependencies. Setting up a virtual environment is a good practice to isolate your Python projects and avoid conflicts between different projects.

To create a virtual environment, open a command prompt or terminal window and run the following command:

```
python -m venv myenv
```

Replace `myenv` with the name of your virtual environment. After creating the virtual environment, you can activate it by running the following command:

On Windows:

```
``` myenv\Scripts\activate
```

On macOS and Linux:

```
source myenv/bin/activate
```

Running Python Code:

Once you have set up your Python environment, you can start writing and running Python code. You can create a new Python script file with a `.py` extension in your code editor and write your Python code in the file.

To run a Python script, you can open a command prompt or terminal window, navigate to the directory where your Python script is located, and run the following command:

```
python script_name.py
```

Replace `script_name.py` with the name of your Python script. The Python interpreter will execute the script, and you will see the output in the command prompt or terminal window.

In conclusion, setting up your Python environment is a straightforward process that involves installing Python, choosing a code editor, installing Python packages, setting
```

up a virtual environment, and running Python code. By following the steps outlined in this article, you can quickly set up your Python environment and start coding in Python. Python is a versatile language that is easy to learn and use, making it an excellent choice for beginners and experienced programmers alike.

Chapter 2: Installing Python in Kali Linux

If you are using Kali Linux, a popular Linux distribution used for penetration testing and ethical hacking, you may want to install Python to take advantage of its capabilities.

Installing Python in Kali Linux is a straightforward process, and in this guide, we will walk you through the steps to do so.

Step 1: Update and Upgrade Kali Linux

Before installing Python, it is recommended to update and upgrade your Kali Linux system to ensure that you have the latest packages and security updates. You can do this by opening a terminal and running the following commands:

sudo apt update sudo apt upgrade

Step 2: Install Python

Kali Linux comes pre-installed with Python 2.7, which is considered to be an older version of Python. To install the latest version of Python (Python 3), you can use the following command:

sudo apt install python3

This command will install Python 3 and its dependencies on your Kali Linux system. Once the installation is complete, you can verify the installation by running the following command:

```
python3 --version
```

This command will display the version of Python 3 installed on your system. Step 3: Install Python Package Manager (pip)
Pip is a package manager for Python that allows you to install and manage Python packages easily. To install pip for Python 3, you can use the following command:

```
sudo apt install python3-pip
```

This command will install pip for Python 3 on your Kali Linux system. Once the installation is complete, you can verify the installation by running the following command:

```
pip3 --version
```

This command will display the version of pip installed on your system. Step 4: Install Virtual Environment (Optional)

A virtual environment is a self-contained directory that contains a specific version of Python and its dependencies. It allows you to work on different projects with different dependencies without affecting the system-wide Python installation. To install virtualenv for Python 3, you can use the following command:

```
sudo apt install python3-venv
```

This command will install virtualenv for Python 3 on your

Kali Linux system. Once the installation is complete, you can create a virtual environment by running the following command:

```
python3 -m venv myenv
```

This command will create a virtual environment named "myenv" in the current directory. To activate the virtual environment, you can run the following command:

```
source myenv/bin/activate
```

This command will activate the virtual environment, and you can install Python packages specific to this environment without affecting the system-wide Python installation.

In conclusion, installing Python in Kali Linux is a simple process that can be done in a few steps. By following the steps outlined in this guide, you can install Python, pip, and virtualenv on your Kali Linux system and start developing Python applications or working on Python projects.

Python is a powerful programming language with a rich ecosystem of libraries and tools, and by installing it on your Kali Linux system, you can leverage its capabilities for various purposes.

Essential Libraries for OSINT in Kali Linux

Open Source Intelligence (OSINT) is a crucial aspect of cybersecurity and threat intelligence. It involves collecting and analyzing information from publicly available sources to gather insights and make informed decisions. In the realm of OSINT, Kali Linux is a popular operating system that comes equipped with a wide range of tools and libraries to aid in the collection and analysis of open-source intelligence.

While Kali Linux provides a plethora of built-in tools for OSINT, there are several essential libraries that can further enhance the capabilities of OSINT practitioners. These libraries offer additional functionalities and features that can streamline the process of gathering and analyzing information from various sources. In this article, we will explore some of the essential libraries for OSINT in Kali Linux.

Recon-ng: Recon-ng is a powerful reconnaissance framework that is built into Kali Linux. It provides a modular approach to conducting OSINT activities, allowing users to gather information from a variety of sources such as social media platforms, public databases, and search engines. Recon-ng comes with a wide range of modules that can be used to perform tasks such as domain reconnaissance, email harvesting, and social media profiling.

Maltego: Maltego is a popular OSINT tool that is widely used for visualizing and analyzing data. It allows users to create interactive graphs that represent relationships between different entities, such as people, organizations, and websites. Maltego can be used to conduct various OSINT activities, including link analysis, social network mapping, and data mining. The tool also supports integration with various data sources, making it a valuable asset for OSINT practitioners.

theHarvester: theHarvester is a versatile OSINT tool that is designed for gathering information from various sources, such as search engines, social media platforms, and public databases. It can be used to collect data on email addresses, domain names, and IP addresses, among other things. theHarvester is highly customizable, allowing users to specify the sources and types of information they want to extract. The tool is particularly useful for conducting reconnaissance on specific targets or organizations.

Shodan: Shodan is a specialized search engine that is focused on indexing internet-connected devices. It allows users to search for specific types of devices, such as webcams, routers, and servers, based on various criteria. Shodan can be used to identify vulnerable devices, conduct reconnaissance on specific networks, and gather information on the internet of things (IoT) ecosystem. The tool provides a wealth of data that can be leveraged for OSINT purposes.

SpiderFoot: SpiderFoot is an open-source OSINT automation tool that is designed to streamline the process of gathering intelligence from multiple sources. It can be used to collect information on domain names, IP addresses, email addresses, and social media profiles, among other things. SpiderFoot automates the process of data collection and analysis, allowing users to focus on interpreting the results and drawing insights from the gathered information. The tool supports integration with various APIs and data sources, making it a valuable asset for OSINT practitioners.

Metagoofil: Metagoofil is a tool that is specifically designed for extracting metadata from public documents, such as PDF files, Word documents, and PowerPoint presentations. It can be used to gather information on the authors, timestamps, and locations of documents, which can be valuable for conducting OSINT investigations.

Metagoofil can also extract embedded URLs and email addresses from documents, providing additional leads for further research. The tool is simple to use and can be a valuable addition to the OSINT toolkit in Kali Linux.

FOCA: FOCA is a powerful metadata analysis tool that is used for extracting information from various file formats, such as PDF files, Word documents, and Excel spreadsheets. It can be used to gather information on the authors, organizations, and timestamps of documents, as well as extract embedded URLs and email addresses. FOCA also provides insights into the structure of websites and networks, allowing users to identify potential vulnerabilities and security risks. The tool is highly customizable and can be tailored to specific OSINT requirements.

In conclusion, these essential libraries for OSINT in Kali Linux can significantly enhance the capabilities of OSINT practitioners by providing additional functionalities and features for gathering and analyzing open-source intelligence. By leveraging these libraries, users can streamline the process of conducting reconnaissance, extracting valuable insights, and making informed decisions based on the gathered information. Incorporating these libraries into the OSINT toolkit in Kali Linux can help enhance the effectiveness and efficiency of OSINT operations.

Setting Up a Virtual Environment

Setting up a virtual environment in a programming language is a crucial step in any software development project. A virtual environment allows developers to create an isolated environment where they can install specific versions of libraries and dependencies without affecting the system-wide installation. This ensures that the project runs smoothly and consistently across different machines.

In this article, we will discuss the importance of setting up a virtual environment in a programming language and provide a step-by-step guide on how to do it.

Why Set Up a Virtual Environment?

Setting up a virtual environment in a programming language offers several benefits. First and foremost, it allows developers to work on multiple projects with different dependencies without worrying about conflicts. For example, if one project requires a specific version of a library while another project requires a different version, a virtual environment can be used to manage these dependencies separately.

Secondly, virtual environments help in maintaining the consistency of the project across different machines. By

27

isolating the project's dependencies, developers can ensure that the code runs the same way on their local machine as it does on a colleague's machine or a production server.

Finally, virtual environments make it easier to manage dependencies and keep them up to date. Instead of installing libraries globally on the system, developers can use a virtual environment to install specific versions of libraries, making it easier to update or roll back dependencies as needed.

Setting Up a Virtual Environment

Setting up a virtual environment in a programming language is a straightforward process. In this guide, we will use Python as an example, but the steps are similar for other programming languages as well.

Install Virtualenv

The first step is to install a virtual environment tool. For Python, the most commonly used tool is virtualenv. To install virtualenv, open a terminal or command prompt and run the following command:

```
```
pip install virtualenv
```
```

Create a New Virtual Environment

Once virtualenv is installed, you can create a new virtual

environment by running the following command:

```
virtualenv myenv
```

This command will create a new directory named `myenv` that contains the virtual environment. You can replace `myenv` with any name you prefer.

Activate the Virtual Environment

To activate the virtual environment, run the following command:

For Windows:

```
myenv\Scripts\activate
```

For Mac and Linux:

```
source myenv/bin/activate
```

After running this command, you will see the name of the virtual environment in the terminal prompt, indicating that the virtual environment is now active.

Install Dependencies

With the virtual environment activated, you can now install the necessary dependencies for your project. For example, if you need to install the `requests` library, you can run the following command:

```
pip install requests
```

This will install the `requests` library within the virtual environment, ensuring that it does not affect the system-wide installation.

Deactivate the Virtual Environment

Once you have finished working on your project, you can deactivate the virtual environment by running the following command:

```
deactivate
```

This will deactivate the virtual environment and return you to the system-wide Python installation.

Setting up a virtual environment in a programming language is an essential step in any software development project. It allows developers to manage dependencies, maintain consistency across different machines, and easily update or roll back dependencies. By following the steps outlined in this guide, you can create a virtual environment for your project and start developing with confidence.

Basic Python for OSINT

Python is a powerful programming language that is widely used in the field of Open Source Intelligence (OSINT). OSINT is the practice of collecting data from publicly available sources to gather information for various purposes such as intelligence gathering, investigations, and research. Python is an ideal language for OSINT due to its simplicity, flexibility, and extensive libraries that can help automate the process of data collection and analysis.

One of the key advantages of using Python for OSINT is its ease of use. Python is known for its readability and simplicity, making it accessible to beginners and experienced programmers alike. The syntax of Python is clear and concise, which makes it easy to learn and understand. This makes it an ideal language for those who are new to programming and want to get started with OSINT.

Python also has a large number of libraries that are specifically designed for data collection and analysis, making it a powerful tool for OSINT practitioners. Some of the most popular libraries for OSINT include Requests, BeautifulSoup, and Scrapy. These libraries allow users to easily scrape data from websites, parse HTML content, and extract information from various sources.

In addition to its libraries, Python also has a wide range of tools and frameworks that can help automate the process of data collection and analysis. For example, tools like Jupyter Notebook and Pandas are commonly used in the field of data science and can be applied to OSINT projects to analyze and visualize data. These tools can help OSINT practitioners to identify patterns, trends, and insights from the data they collect.

Another advantage of using Python for OSINT is its versatility. Python can be used for a wide range of tasks, from web scraping and data analysis to building web applications and automating tasks. This flexibility makes Python a valuable tool for OSINT practitioners who need to adapt to different types of projects and data sources.

To get started with Python for OSINT, it is important to have a basic understanding of the language and its key concepts. Some of the fundamental concepts of Python include variables, data types, loops, and functions.
Variables are used to store data, while data types define the type of data that can be stored in a variable. Loops are used to iterate over a sequence of data, while functions are used to encapsulate code and make it reusable.

In addition to these basic concepts, it is also important to understand how to work with libraries and tools in Python. Libraries are pre-written code that can be imported into a Python script to extend its functionality. Tools like Requests and BeautifulSoup can be used to collect data from websites, while tools like Pandas and Matplotlib can be used to analyze and visualize data.

Overall, Python is an excellent language for OSINT due to its simplicity, flexibility, and extensive libraries. By learning the basics of Python and exploring its libraries and tools, OSINT practitioners can automate the process of data collection and analysis, making their work more efficient and effective. Whether you are new to programming or an experienced coder, Python is a valuable tool for anyone working in the field of Open Source Intelligence.

Chapter 3: Python Fundamentals

Python is a high-level, interpreted programming language known for its simplicity and readability. It was created by Guido van Rossum in the late 1980s and has since become one of the most popular programming languages in the world. Python is used for a wide range of applications, including web development, data analysis, artificial intelligence, and scientific computing.

One of the key features of Python is its readability. The language is designed to be easy to read and write, with a clean and simple syntax that makes it accessible to beginners and experienced programmers alike. This readability is achieved through the use of indentation to define code blocks, rather than relying on curly braces or keywords like "end" or "fi" as in other languages.

Python is also known for its versatility. It supports multiple programming paradigms, including procedural, object-oriented, and functional programming. This flexibility allows developers to choose the best approach for each project, making Python a powerful tool for a wide range of applications.

Another key feature of Python is its extensive standard library. Python comes with a large collection of modules and packages that provide ready-made solutions for common programming tasks, such as working with files, networking, and data processing. This makes it easy for developers to quickly build complex applications without having to reinvent the wheel.

Python's dynamic typing and automatic memory management make it a highly productive language for developers. Dynamic typing means that variables do not need to be explicitly declared with a data type, allowing for more flexible and concise code. Automatic memory management, through the use of garbage collection, frees developers from having to manage memory manually, reducing the risk of memory leaks and other common programming errors.

Python is also known for its strong community support. The Python community is large and active, with a wealth of resources available to help developers learn and grow. Online forums, tutorials, and documentation make it easy to find answers to questions and troubleshoot issues, while conferences and meetups provide opportunities for networking and collaboration.

In addition to its core features, Python has a number of advanced capabilities that make it a popular choice for data analysis and scientific computing. The NumPy and SciPy libraries provide powerful tools for working with arrays, matrices, and other mathematical structures, while the pandas library offers data manipulation and analysis tools that are essential for working with large datasets.

Python's support for machine learning and artificial intelligence has also made it a popular choice for developers working in these fields. The scikit-learn library provides a wide range of machine learning algorithms that can be easily integrated into Python applications, while TensorFlow and PyTorch are popular frameworks for building and training deep learning models.

Overall, Python is a versatile and powerful programming language that is well-suited to a wide range of applications. Its simplicity, readability, and extensive standard library make it an ideal choice for beginners and experienced developers alike, while its advanced capabilities in data analysis, scientific computing, and artificial intelligence make it a valuable tool for tackling complex problems in a variety of fields. Whether you're just starting out in programming or looking to expand your skill set, Python is a language that is worth learning and mastering.

Data Structures and File Handling – Python

Data structures and file handling are essential components of programming in Python. Understanding how to work with data structures and manipulate files is crucial for building efficient and scalable applications. In this article, we will explore the basics of data structures and file handling in Python, and discuss some common techniques and best practices.

Data Structures in Python:

Data structures are used to store and organize data in a way that makes it easy to access and manipulate. Python provides several built-in data structures that are commonly used in programming, including lists, tuples, dictionaries, and sets.

Lists are one of the most versatile data structures in

Python. They are ordered collections of items that can be of different data types. Lists are mutable, which means that you can add, remove, or modify elements in a list. Here's an example of how to create a list in Python:

```python
my_list = [1, 2, 3, 4, 5]
```

Tuples are similar to lists, but they are immutable, which means that once a tuple is created, its elements cannot be changed. Tuples are often used to represent fixed collections of items. Here's an example of how to create a tuple in Python:

```python
my_tuple = (1, 2, 3, 4, 5)
```

Dictionaries are another important data structure in Python. They are collections of key-value pairs, where each key is unique and maps to a corresponding value. Dictionaries are unordered, which means that the order of elements in a dictionary is not guaranteed. Here's an example of how to create a dictionary in Python:

```python
my_dict = {'a': 1, 'b': 2, 'c': 3}
```

Sets are collections of unique elements that are unordered. Sets are useful for performing operations such as union, intersection, and difference between two sets. Here's an example of how to create a set in Python:

```python
my_set = {1, 2, 3, 4, 5}
```

File Handling in Python:

File handling is the process of working with files on a computer. Python provides built-in functions and modules for reading from and writing to files. File handling is important for tasks such as reading input data, writing output data, and storing information persistently.

To open a file in Python, you can use the `open()` function, which takes two arguments: the file name and the mode in which to open the file. The mode can be 'r' for reading, 'w' for writing, 'a' for appending, or 'r+' for reading and writing. Here's an example of how to open a file for reading:

```python
file = open('example.txt', 'r')
```

Once a file is opened, you can read its contents using the `read()` method, which reads the entire file as a single string. You can also use the `readline()` method to read one line at a time, or the `readlines()` method to read all lines into a list. Here's an example of how to read from a file in Python:

```python
```

```
content = file.read() print(content)
```

To write to a file in Python, you can use the `write()` method, which writes a string to the file. You can also use the `writelines()` method to write a list of strings to the file. Here's an example of how to write to a file in Python:

```python
file = open('example.txt', 'w') file.write('Hello, world!')
file.close()
```

It's important to always close a file after you are done working with it, to release system resources and ensure that changes are saved to the file. You can use the `close()` method to close a file in Python.

In addition to reading and writing files, Python also provides modules for working with different file formats, such as CSV, JSON, and XML. These modules make it easy to parse and manipulate files in specific formats, and are commonly used in data processing and analysis tasks.

Best Practices for Data Structures and File Handling in Python:

When working with data structures and file handling in Python, there are several best practices that can help you write efficient and maintainable code:

Use built-in data structures: Python provides a rich set of built-in data structures that are optimized for performance and memory usage. Whenever possible, use built-in data structures such as lists, tuples, dictionaries, and sets, instead of implementing custom data structures.

Choose the right data structure for the task: Different data structures have different strengths and weaknesses.

Choose the data structure that best fits the requirements of your program, based on factors such as access patterns, size of data, and complexity of operations.

Use list comprehensions: List comprehensions are a concise and expressive way to create lists in Python.

Working with APIs And Python

Application Programming Interfaces (APIs) have revolutionized the way software applications communicate with each other. APIs allow different software systems to interact with each other seamlessly, enabling developers to access and manipulate data from various sources. Python, with its simplicity and versatility, has become a popular choice for working with APIs due to its ease of use and extensive library support.

In this article, we will explore how to work with APIs using Python, covering the basics of API integration, making API requests, handling responses, and parsing data. We will also discuss some common use cases for working with APIs in Python and provide examples to help you get started.

What is an API?

An API is a set of rules and protocols that allows different software applications to communicate with each other. APIs define the methods and data formats that applications can use to request and exchange information. APIs can be used to access data from external sources, such as web services, databases, or other software applications.

There are different types of APIs, including RESTful APIs, SOAP APIs, and GraphQL APIs. RESTful APIs are the most common type of API and are widely used for web applications. RESTful APIs use HTTP methods, such as GET, POST, PUT, and DELETE, to perform operations on resources.

How to work with APIs in Python

Python provides several libraries for working with APIs, including requests, urllib, and httplib. The requests library is the most popular choice for making HTTP requests in Python due to its simplicity and ease of use. To install the requests library, you can use pip, the Python package manager:

```bash
pip install requests
```

Once you have installed the requests library, you can start making API requests in Python. The requests library provides a simple and intuitive API for making HTTP requests and handling responses. Here is an example of how to make a GET request to a RESTful API using the requests library:

```python
import requests

url = 'https://api.example.com/data' response = requests.get(url)

if response.status_code == 200: data = response.json() print(data)

else:
print('Failed to fetch data:', response.status_code)
```

In this example, we import the requests library and make a GET request to the specified URL. We then check the status code of the response to ensure that the request was successful. If the status code is 200 (OK), we parse the JSON data in the response and print it to the console. Otherwise, we print an error message indicating that the request failed.

Handling API responses in Python

When working with APIs in Python, it is important to handle API responses properly to ensure that your application behaves correctly. API responses can contain various types of data, such as JSON, XML, or plain text, and you may need to parse the response data accordingly.

The requests library provides built-in support for parsing

JSON and XML data in API responses. If the API response contains JSON data, you can use the .json() method to parse the JSON data and convert it into a Python dictionary. If the API response contains XML data, you can use the ElementTree module in the Python standard library to parse the XML data.

Here is an example of how to parse JSON data in an API response using the requests library:

```python
import requests

url = 'https://api.example.com/data'
response = requests.get(url)

if response.status_code == 200:
    data = response.json()
    print(data)
else:
    print('Failed to fetch data:', response.status_code)
```

In this example, we make a GET request to the specified URL and parse the JSON data in the response using the .json() method. We then print the parsed data to the console. If the request fails, we print an error message indicating the status code of the response.

Common use cases for working with APIs in Python

There are many use cases for working with APIs in Python, ranging from accessing data from external sources to automating repetitive tasks. Some common use cases for working with APIs in Python include:

43

Data retrieval: APIs allow you to access data from external sources, such as web services, databases, or other software applications. You can use APIs to retrieve data for analysis, visualization, or reporting in your Python applications.

Automation: APIs can be used to automate repetitive tasks, such as sending emails, updating databases, or posting to social media. You can use APIs to interact with various online services and automate workflows in your Python scripts.

Integration: APIs enable different software systems to communicate with each other, allowing you to integrate data and functionality from multiple sources. You can use APIs to integrate third-party services, such as payment gateways, messaging platforms, or mapping services, into your Python applications.

Testing: APIs are commonly used for testing software applications, as they provide a standardized way to interact with the application's functionality.

Introduction to Web Scraping

Web scraping is a powerful technique used to extract data from websites. It involves automating the process of collecting information from the web by writing scripts or programs that simulate human browsing behavior. This allows users to gather data from multiple sources quickly and efficiently, without the need for manual copying and pasting.

There are many reasons why someone might want to use web scraping. For businesses, web scraping can be a valuable tool for market research, competitor analysis, lead generation, and monitoring of online reputation. For researchers, web scraping can be used to collect data for academic studies, analyze trends, and gather information for a variety of purposes. And for individuals, web scraping can be used to extract information such as product prices, reviews, and contact details.

Web scraping can be done using a variety of programming languages, but one of the most popular languages for this purpose is Python. Python is a versatile and beginner-friendly language that is well-suited for web scraping because of its rich library ecosystem and ease of use. In this article, we will provide an introduction to web scraping in Python, covering the basics of how to get started, common tools and libraries used, and best practices to follow.

Getting Started with Web Scraping in Python

To get started with web scraping in Python, you will need to install a few libraries that are commonly used for this purpose. The most popular library for web scraping in Python is BeautifulSoup, which is a powerful library for parsing HTML and XML documents. Another commonly used library is requests, which is used to send HTTP requests and retrieve web pages.

To install these libraries, you can use the pip package manager, which comes pre-installed with Python. Simply open a terminal or command prompt and run the following commands:

pip install beautifulsoup4 pip install requests

Once you have installed these libraries, you can start writing your web scraping scripts. The first step in web scraping is to retrieve the HTML content of the webpage you want to scrape. This can be done using the requests library, which allows you to send an HTTP request to the webpage and retrieve the response. Here is an example of how to retrieve the HTML content of a webpage using requests:

import requests

url = 'https://www.example.com' response = requests.get(url) html_content = response.text

Once you have retrieved the HTML content of the webpage, you can use BeautifulSoup to parse the content and extract the information you need.

BeautifulSoup allows you to navigate the HTML document using methods like find() and find_all() to locate specific elements on the page. Here is an example of how to extract all the links on a webpage using BeautifulSoup: from bs4 import BeautifulSoup

soup = BeautifulSoup(html_content, 'html.parser') links = soup.find_all('a')

for link in links:
print(link.get('href'))

Common Tools and Libraries for Web Scraping in Python

In addition to BeautifulSoup and requests, there are several other tools and libraries that are commonly used for web scraping in Python. One popular tool is Scrapy, which is a powerful and flexible web scraping framework that allows you to build web scrapers quickly and efficiently. Scrapy provides a high-level API for web scraping and includes features like automatic handling of cookies, form submissions, and pagination.

Another useful library for web scraping in Python is Selenium, which is a web automation tool that allows you to control a web browser programmatically. Selenium is particularly useful for scraping websites that use JavaScript, as it allows you to interact with the webpage as a human user would. Selenium can be used in conjunction with BeautifulSoup or Scrapy to scrape dynamic websites or websites that require user interaction.

Best Practices for Web Scraping in Python

When web scraping, it is important to follow best practices to ensure that your scraping activities are ethical and legal. Here are some best practices to keep in mind when web scraping in Python:

Respect the website's terms of service: Before scraping a website, make sure to read and understand the website's terms of service. Some websites explicitly prohibit web scraping, so it is important to respect their policies and not violate their terms of use.

Use a user-agent string: When sending HTTP requests to a website, it is a good practice to include a user-agent string in the request headers. This identifies your scraper to the website and allows the website to track and block malicious bots.

Limit the frequency of requests: To avoid overloading a website's servers, it is important to limit the frequency of your requests. Make sure to space out your requests and avoid sending too many requests in a short period of time.

Monitor your scraping activities: Keep track of your scraping activities and monitor the performance of your scripts. If you notice any issues or errors, make sure to address them promptly to avoid getting blocked by the website.

Be respectful and ethical: Finally, always be respectful and ethical in your web scraping activities.

Chapter 4: Understanding Web Scraping

Web scraping is a technique used to extract data from websites. It involves automating the process of gathering information from web pages and saving it in a structured format for further analysis. Web scraping can be used for a variety of purposes, such as market research, competitive analysis, and data mining.

To understand web scraping, it is important to first understand how websites are structured. Websites are built using HTML, CSS, and JavaScript. HTML is used to create the structure of the web page, CSS is used to style the page, and JavaScript is used to add interactivity. When you visit a website, your web browser sends a request to the server hosting the website, which then sends back the HTML, CSS, and JavaScript code that makes up the page.

Web scraping involves sending a request to a website and extracting the HTML code that makes up the page. This code can then be parsed to extract the data that you are interested in. There are several tools and libraries available that can help with web scraping, such as BeautifulSoup, Scrapy, and Selenium.

One of the key challenges of web scraping is dealing with the structure of the website. Websites are constantly changing, and the HTML code that makes up a page can be complex and difficult to parse. In addition, websites may have measures in place to prevent scraping, such as CAPTCHAs or rate limiting.

There are several different approaches to web scraping, depending on the complexity of the website and the amount of data that needs to be extracted. One common approach is to use XPath or CSS selectors to identify the elements on the page that contain the data you are interested in. Another approach is to use regular expressions to extract data from the HTML code.

Web scraping can be a powerful tool for gathering data from the web, but it is important to be mindful of the legal and ethical implications of scraping. Some websites have terms of service that prohibit scraping, and scraping large amounts of data from a website can put a strain on the server hosting the site. It is important to respect the terms of service of the websites you are scraping and to be considerate of the impact that scraping can have on the website.

In conclusion, web scraping is a valuable technique for extracting data from websites. By understanding the structure of websites and using the right tools and techniques, you can gather the data you need for analysis and research. However, it is important to be mindful of the legal and ethical implications of scraping and to respect the terms of service of the websites you are scraping. With the right approach, web scraping can be a powerful tool for gathering valuable insights from the web.

HTML and CSS Basics

HTML (Hypertext Markup Language) and CSS (Cascading Style Sheets) are two essential languages used in web development. HTML is used to create the structure and content of a webpage, while CSS is used to style and format the webpage. Understanding the basics of HTML and CSS is crucial for anyone looking to build websites or work in the field of web development.

HTML is a markup language that uses tags to define the structure of a webpage. Tags are enclosed in angle brackets and come in pairs, with an opening tag and a closing tag. The opening tag is used to define the beginning of an element, while the closing tag is used to define the end of an element. For example, the

tag is used to define a paragraph, with the opening tag and the closing tag

.

HTML elements can also have attributes that provide additional information about the element. Attributes are placed inside the opening tag and are written as name-value pairs. For example, the tag is used to insert an image into a webpage and has attributes such as src (source) and alt (alternative text). The src attribute specifies the URL of the image file, while the alt attribute provides a text description of the image.

CSS is a style sheet language used to control the presentation of a webpage. CSS allows developers to style elements such as text, images, and layout, making the webpage visually appealing and user-friendly. CSS can be applied to HTML elements using selectors, properties, and values.

Selectors are used to target specific HTML elements that you want to style. There are different types of selectors, such as element selectors, class selectors, and ID selectors. Element selectors target specific HTML elements, while class selectors target elements with a specific class attribute, and ID selectors target elements with a specific ID attribute.

Properties are used to define the style of an element, such as color, font size, and background color. Values are assigned to properties to specify the desired style. For example, the color property can be set to a specific color value, such as red or #FF0000.

CSS can be applied to HTML elements in three ways: inline, internal, and external. Inline CSS is applied directly to an HTML element using the style attribute. Internal CSS is placed within the element in the head section of an HTML document. External CSS is stored in a separate CSS file and linked to the HTML document using the element.

When building a webpage, it is important to use a combination of HTML and CSS to create a well-structured and visually appealing design. By understanding the basics of HTML and CSS, developers can create websites that are functional, responsive, and easy to navigate.

In conclusion, HTML and CSS are essential languages for web development. HTML is used to create the structure and content of a webpage, while CSS is used to style and format the webpage. By mastering the basics of HTML and CSS, developers can create websites that are visually appealing, user-friendly, and responsive.

Whether you are a beginner or an experienced developer, understanding HTML and CSS is crucial for building successful websites.

Navigating the DOM

Navigating the DOM (Document Object Model) is a fundamental aspect of web development. The DOM is a representation of the structure of a web page, allowing developers to manipulate and interact with its elements using JavaScript. Understanding how to navigate the DOM is crucial for building dynamic and interactive websites.

When working with the DOM, developers can access and manipulate elements such as text, images, forms, and more. By understanding how to navigate the DOM, developers can create responsive and engaging web applications that enhance the user experience.

One of the key concepts of navigating the DOM is the use of methods such as getElementById, getElementsByClassName, and querySelector. These methods allow developers to target specific elements on a web page based on their unique identifiers, classes, or selectors.

For example, the getElementById method allows developers to select an element by its ID attribute. This is useful for targeting specific elements on a page, such as a form input field or a button. Similarly, the getElementsByClassName method allows developers to select elements based on their class attribute, making it easy to apply styles or functionality to multiple elements at once.

The querySelector method is another powerful tool for navigating the DOM. This method allows developers to select elements using CSS selectors, providing a flexible and intuitive way to target elements on a page. For example, developers can use querySelector to select all input fields within a form or all elements with a specific class name.

In addition to selecting elements, developers can also navigate the DOM by accessing and manipulating element properties and attributes. For example, developers can change the text content of an element using the innerText or innerHTML properties, or update the value of an input field using the value property.

Another important concept in navigating the DOM is traversing the DOM tree. The DOM tree is a hierarchical structure that represents the relationship between elements on a web page. By understanding how to traverse the DOM tree, developers can move between parent, child, and sibling elements to access and manipulate specific parts of a page.

For example, developers can use methods such as

parentNode, firstChild, lastChild, nextSibling, and previousSibling to navigate the DOM tree. These methods allow developers to move up, down, and across the DOM tree to access and manipulate elements as needed.

In addition to selecting and traversing elements, developers can also create new elements and append them to the DOM. This is useful for dynamically adding content to a page, such as new paragraphs, images, or buttons. By creating elements using methods such as createElement and appendChild, developers can enhance the interactivity and functionality of a web page.

Overall, navigating the DOM is a crucial skill for web developers. By understanding how to select, traverse, and manipulate elements on a web page, developers can create dynamic and interactive websites that engage users and enhance the user experience. Whether you are a beginner or an experienced developer, mastering the art of navigating the DOM is essential for building modern and responsive web applications.

Advanced Web Scraping Techniques

Web scraping is a powerful technique used to extract data from websites. While basic web scraping techniques are relatively easy to implement, advanced web scraping techniques require a deeper understanding of how websites are structured and how to navigate around potential obstacles such as anti-scraping measures. In this article, we will explore some advanced web scraping techniques that can help you extract data more efficiently and effectively.

Using Headless Browsers

One of the most common challenges in web scraping is dealing with websites that use JavaScript to dynamically load content. Traditional web scraping libraries like BeautifulSoup and Scrapy are not able to execute JavaScript, which means that they may not be able to scrape all the data on a website. One way to overcome this limitation is to use a headless browser like Selenium or Puppeteer.

Headless browsers are essentially web browsers that do not have a graphical user interface, allowing them to run in the background and interact with websites just like a regular browser. By using a headless browser, you can simulate user interactions with the website, such as clicking buttons and scrolling down the page, to ensure that all the content is loaded before scraping it.

Handling Dynamic Content

In addition to using headless browsers, another advanced technique for scraping websites with dynamic content is to monitor network requests. When a website loads content dynamically, it often makes requests to the server for additional data. By monitoring these network requests, you can identify the URLs that the website is requesting and extract the data directly from the API endpoints.

Tools like Chrome Developer Tools or Burp Suite can help you monitor network requests and analyze the data being sent and received. Once you have identified the API endpoints, you can use a library like Requests or Axios to send HTTP requests to these endpoints and extract the data you need.

Dealing with Anti-Scraping Measures

Many websites employ anti-scraping measures to prevent automated bots from accessing their content. These measures can include CAPTCHAs, IP blocking, user-agent detection, and rate limiting. To bypass these anti-scraping measures, you may need to use techniques like rotating IP addresses, changing user agents, and implementing delays between requests.

One common anti-scraping measure is CAPTCHA, which requires users to solve a challenge to prove that they are human. To bypass CAPTCHAs, you can use services like Anti-CAPTCHA or 2Captcha, which provide APIs for solving CAPTCHAs automatically. Another technique is to use a CAPTCHA-solving browser extension like Buster or Rumola, which can automatically solve CAPTCHAs as you browse the web.

Scraping Multiple Pages

When scraping websites with multiple pages, it can be tedious to manually navigate through each page and extract the data. One advanced technique for scraping multiple pages is to use pagination techniques like next page links or infinite scrolling. By identifying the pattern of pagination on the website, you can automate the process of navigating through each page and extracting the data.

For websites with next page links, you can use a loop to iterate through each page and extract the data. For websites with infinite scrolling, you can use a headless browser to simulate scrolling down the page until all the content is loaded. By automating the process of navigating through multiple pages, you can scrape large amounts of data more efficiently.

Data Cleaning and Transformation

Once you have extracted the data from a website, you may need to clean and transform the data before using it for analysis or visualization. This process can involve removing duplicates, correcting errors, standardizing formats, and aggregating data from multiple sources. Advanced web scraping techniques like regular expressions, data manipulation libraries, and data cleaning tools can help you clean and transform the data more effectively.

Regular expressions are a powerful tool for extracting specific patterns from text data. By using regular expressions, you can search for and replace text patterns, extract specific values, and validate data formats. Data manipulation libraries like Pandas or NumPy can help you clean and transform tabular data, such as removing missing values, converting data types, and aggregating data. Data cleaning tools like OpenRefine or Trifacta can help you clean and transform messy data sets with interactive visualizations and automated cleaning operations.

Monitoring and Error Handling

When scraping websites, it is important to monitor the scraping process and handle errors gracefully. Monitoring the scraping process can help you identify issues like slow response times, broken links, and changes in website structure. By logging the scraping process and setting up alerts for errors, you can ensure that your scraping script runs smoothly and efficiently.

Error handling is another important aspect of web scraping, as websites can sometimes return unexpected responses or encounter errors. By implementing try-except blocks and handling exceptions, you can prevent your scraping script from crashing and continue scraping even when errors occur. Additionally, you can use techniques like retrying failed requests, logging errors, and saving partial results to ensure that you do not lose any data during the scraping process.

Chapter 5: Handling JavaScript-Rendered Content

Handling JavaScript-rendered content in any programming language can be a challenging task as it requires a deep understanding of how JavaScript works and how it interacts with the DOM (Document Object Model). In this article, we will discuss some tips and tricks for effectively handling JavaScript-rendered content in any programming language.

First and foremost, it is important to understand how JavaScript works and how it manipulates the DOM. JavaScript is a client-side scripting language that is used to add interactivity and dynamic behavior to web pages. When a web page is loaded, the browser parses the HTML and CSS to create the DOM, which is a tree-like structure that represents the structure of the web page. JavaScript can then be used to manipulate the DOM by adding, removing, or modifying elements on the page.

One common challenge when handling JavaScript-rendered content is that the content may not be immediately available when the page is loaded. This is because JavaScript can be used to dynamically load content after the page has been loaded. In order to handle this, you may need to wait for the content to be fully loaded before accessing it. This can be done using techniques such as waiting for a specific element to appear on the page or using a timeout to wait for a certain amount of time before accessing the content.

Another challenge when handling JavaScript-rendered content is that the content may be loaded asynchronously, meaning that it may not be loaded in the order that it appears in the HTML. This can make it difficult to access the content in the correct order. One way to handle this is to use promises or callbacks to ensure that the content is loaded in the correct order before accessing it.

In addition to handling asynchronous content, you may also need to handle content that is loaded dynamically through AJAX requests. AJAX (Asynchronous JavaScript and XML) is a technique that allows web pages to update content without reloading the entire page. When handling JavaScript-rendered content that is loaded through AJAX requests, you may need to listen for events that indicate when the content has been loaded and then access the content once it is available.

When handling JavaScript-rendered content in any programming language, it is important to consider the performance implications of the code. JavaScript can be a resource-intensive language, especially when manipulating the DOM or making AJAX requests. In order to optimize performance, you may need to minimize the number of DOM manipulations and AJAX requests, cache content that is frequently accessed, and use techniques such as lazy loading to defer the loading of content until it is needed.

Overall, handling JavaScript-rendered content in any programming language requires a solid understanding of how JavaScript works and how it interacts with the DOM. By using techniques such as waiting for content to be fully loaded, handling asynchronous content, and optimizing performance, you can effectively handle JavaScript-rendered content in any programming language.

Using Selenium for Dynamic Content

Selenium is a powerful tool that is widely used for automating web browsers. It is particularly useful for testing websites and web applications, as it allows developers to simulate user interactions and verify the functionality of their code. One of the key features of Selenium is its ability to handle dynamic content on web pages.

Dynamic content refers to elements on a web page that change or update without the need for a full page reload. This can include things like pop-up windows, sliders, animations, and live updates. These elements can present a challenge for automated testing, as traditional testing tools may not be able to interact with them properly.

Selenium, however, is well-equipped to handle dynamic content. It provides a range of methods and functions that allow developers to interact with these elements and test their functionality. In this article, we will explore some of the ways in which Selenium can be used to work with dynamic content on web pages.

One of the key features of Selenium is its ability to wait for elements to appear on a page before interacting with them. This is particularly useful for dynamic content, as it ensures that the test script does not try to interact with an element before it has fully loaded. Selenium provides a range of wait commands, such as WebDriverWait and FluentWait, which allow developers to specify a maximum time to wait for an element to appear.

Another useful feature of Selenium is its ability to handle alerts and pop-up windows. Many websites use pop-ups to display important information or to prompt the user for input. Selenium provides methods for handling these pop-ups, such as switchTo().alert() and switchTo().window(), which allow developers to interact with the content of the pop-up window.

Selenium also provides methods for working with iframes, which are often used to embed content from other sources on a web page. By using the switchTo().frame() method, developers can switch the focus of the Selenium driver to a specific iframe and interact with its content.

In addition to these features, Selenium also provides methods for working with dynamic elements such as sliders and dropdown menus. By using the Actions class, developers can simulate user interactions such as dragging and dropping elements or selecting options from a dropdown menu.

Overall, Selenium is a powerful tool for working with dynamic content on web pages. Its range of methods and functions make it easy to interact with a wide variety of elements, ensuring that your automated tests are comprehensive and effective. By using Selenium to test dynamic content, developers can ensure that their websites and web applications are functioning correctly and providing a seamless user experience.

In conclusion, Selenium is an invaluable tool for working with dynamic content on web pages. Its range of features and functions make it easy to interact with a wide variety of elements, ensuring that your automated tests are comprehensive and effective. By using Selenium to test dynamic content, developers can ensure that their websites and web applications are functioning correctly and providing a seamless user experience.

Scraping APIs with Python

In today's digital age, data is king. From social media platforms to e-commerce websites, businesses and individuals alike rely on data to make informed decisions and drive growth. One of the most common ways to access data from various sources is through Application Programming Interfaces (APIs). APIs allow developers to access and retrieve data from a server or application in a structured and organized manner.

Python is a popular programming language among developers for its simplicity and versatility. With Python, developers can easily interact with APIs to retrieve data and perform various tasks. In this article, we will explore how to scrape APIs with Python and leverage the power of data to drive business decisions.

What is API Scraping?

API scraping refers to the process of extracting data from an API using automated scripts or tools. APIs provide a structured way to access data from various sources, such as social media platforms, e-commerce websites, and government databases. By scraping APIs, developers can retrieve specific data sets, manipulate the data, and analyze it for insights.

Scraping APIs with Python allows developers to automate the data retrieval process and extract large volumes of data quickly and efficiently. Python libraries such as requests and BeautifulSoup make it easy to interact with APIs and parse the retrieved data.

How to Scrape APIs with Python

To scrape APIs with Python, developers need to follow a few simple steps:

Identify the API endpoint: The first step in scraping an API is to identify the API endpoint, which is the URL that developers can use to access the data. The API endpoint typically includes parameters that developers can use to filter and retrieve specific data sets.

Make a request to the API: Once developers have identified the API endpoint, they can use the requests library in Python to make a request to the API. The requests library allows developers to send HTTP requests to the API and retrieve the response data.

Parse the response data: After making a request to the API, developers need to parse the response data to extract the relevant information. The BeautifulSoup library in Python is a powerful tool for parsing HTML and XML data structures. Developers can use BeautifulSoup to extract specific data elements from the API response.

Analyze and manipulate the data: Once developers have extracted the data from the API response, they can analyze and manipulate the data to derive insights. Python libraries such as pandas and NumPy make it easy to perform data analysis and visualization tasks.

Example of API Scraping with Python

To demonstrate how to scrape APIs with Python, let's consider an example of scraping weather data from the OpenWeatherMap API. The OpenWeatherMap API provides access to weather data for various locations around the world.

First, developers need to sign up for an API key on the OpenWeatherMap website. The API key is a unique identifier that developers can use to authenticate their requests to the API.

Next, developers can use the requests library in Python to make a request to the OpenWeatherMap API and retrieve weather data for a specific location. The following code snippet demonstrates how to make a request to the OpenWeatherMap API and retrieve weather data for New York City:

```python
python import requests

api_key = 'YOUR_API_KEY' city = 'New York'
url                                                =
f'http://api.openweathermap.org/data/2.5/weather?q={cit
```

```
y}&appid={api_key}'

response = requests.get(url) data = response.json()

print(data)
```

In this code snippet, developers need to replace 'YOUR_API_KEY' with their actual API key from the OpenWeatherMap website. The code makes a GET request to the OpenWeatherMap API with the specified city parameter and API key. The response data is then converted to a JSON format using the `json()` method.

Developers can then parse the JSON data to extract specific weather information, such as temperature, humidity, and wind speed. They can also analyze the data and visualize it using Python libraries such as matplotlib and seaborn.

Best Practices for API Scraping with Python

When scraping APIs with Python, developers should follow best practices to ensure efficient and ethical data retrieval:

Respect API rate limits: Many APIs impose rate limits on the number of requests developers can make within a specific time frame. Developers should adhere to these rate limits to avoid being blocked by the API provider.

Use caching: To minimize the number of requests to the API, developers can implement caching mechanisms to store and reuse previously retrieved data. Caching can improve performance and reduce the load on the API server.

Handle errors gracefully: API requests can fail due to various reasons, such as network issues or server errors. Developers should implement error handling mechanisms to gracefully handle failed requests and retry them if necessary.

Monitor API usage: Developers should monitor their API usage and track the number of requests made to the API. Monitoring API usage can help developers identify potential issues and optimize their scraping scripts.

Data Extraction with BeautifulSoup – python

Data extraction is a crucial aspect of web scraping, which involves extracting data from websites and storing it in a structured format for further analysis. BeautifulSoup is a popular Python library used for parsing HTML and XML documents, making it easier to extract data from web pages.

In this article, we will explore how to use BeautifulSoup for data extraction in Python and discuss its various features and capabilities.

What is BeautifulSoup?

BeautifulSoup is a Python library that is used for parsing HTML and XML documents. It provides a simple and intuitive way to navigate and search through the document's structure, making it easier to extract specific data elements.

BeautifulSoup is widely used for web scraping tasks, as it allows developers to extract data from websites in a structured format. It provides various methods and functions for navigating and searching through the document's hierarchy, making it easier to extract data based on specific criteria.

How to install BeautifulSoup?

Before we can start using BeautifulSoup for data extraction, we need to install the library. BeautifulSoup can be installed using pip, the Python package manager. To install BeautifulSoup, run the following command in your terminal:

pip install beautifulsoup4

Once the installation is complete, we can start using BeautifulSoup for data extraction in Python. Basic data extraction with BeautifulSoup
To demonstrate how to use BeautifulSoup for data extraction, let's consider a simple example. Suppose we have a web page containing a list of products, each with a title, price, and description. Our goal is to extract this data and store it in a structured format for further analysis.

First, we need to import the necessary libraries:

```python
from bs4 import BeautifulSoup import requests
```

Next, we need to fetch the web page content using the requests library:

```python
url = 'https://example.com/products' response = requests.get(url)
```

Now, we can create a BeautifulSoup object and parse the HTML content of the web page:

```python
soup = BeautifulSoup(response.content, 'html.parser')
```

Once we have created the BeautifulSoup object, we can start extracting data from the web page. We can use various methods and functions provided by BeautifulSoup to navigate and search through the document's structure.

For example, to extract the titles of all products on the page, we can use the find_all method to find all elements with a specific class:

```python
titles = soup.find_all('h2', class_='product-title') for title in titles:
print(title.text)
```

Similarly, we can extract the prices and descriptions of the products by finding elements with the corresponding classes:

```python
prices = soup.find_all('span', class_='product-price')
descriptions = soup.find_all('p', class_='product-description')
```

By using BeautifulSoup's navigation and search capabilities, we can extract the desired data elements from the web page and store them in a structured format for further analysis.

Advanced data extraction with BeautifulSoup

In addition to basic data extraction, BeautifulSoup provides various advanced features and capabilities for handling more complex web scraping tasks. Some of the advanced techniques that can be used with BeautifulSoup include:

Navigating the document's hierarchy: BeautifulSoup allows developers to navigate the document's hierarchy using methods like find, find_all, find_next, find_previous, etc. These methods make it easier to locate specific elements within the document based on various criteria.

Working with CSS selectors: BeautifulSoup supports CSS selectors, which can be used to select elements based on their CSS properties. This allows developers to extract data more efficiently by targeting specific elements using

CSS selectors.

Handling different types of data: BeautifulSoup can handle various types of data, including HTML, XML, and

other document formats. This makes it a versatile tool for extracting data from different types of web pages.

Handling dynamic content: BeautifulSoup can handle dynamic content generated by JavaScript or other client-side technologies. This allows developers to extract data from web pages that contain dynamic elements or content loaded asynchronously.

Error handling: BeautifulSoup provides error handling mechanisms to handle exceptions and errors that may occur during data extraction. This ensures that the scraping process is robust and reliable, even in the presence of unexpected issues.

By leveraging these advanced features and capabilities of BeautifulSoup, developers can extract data more efficiently and effectively from web pages, making it easier to perform data analysis and other tasks.

Best practices for data extraction with BeautifulSoup

When using BeautifulSoup for data extraction, it is important to follow best practices to ensure that the scraping process is efficient, reliable, and respectful of the website's terms of service. Some best practices for data extraction with BeautifulSoup include:

Respect robots.txt: Before scraping a website, check its robots.txt file to see if web scraping is allowed. Respect the website's terms of service and avoid scraping pages that are explicitly disallowed.

Use headers and user agents: When sending requests to a website, include headers and user agents to identify the scraping bot as a legitimate user agent. This helps prevent the scraping bot from being blocked by the

Chapter 6: Installing and Using BeautifulSoup

BeautifulSoup is a Python library that is used for web scraping. It allows you to easily extract data from HTML and XML files, making it a valuable tool for anyone who needs to gather information from websites. In this article, we will discuss how to install and use BeautifulSoup in Python.

Installing BeautifulSoup is a simple process. The library can be installed using pip, which is the package installer for Python. To install BeautifulSoup, open a terminal window and type the following command:

```
pip install beautifulsoup4
```

This command will download and install the latest version of BeautifulSoup from the Python Package Index (PyPI). Once the installation is complete, you can start using BeautifulSoup in your Python scripts.

To use BeautifulSoup in your Python scripts, you first need to import the library. You can do this by adding the following line of code at the beginning of your script:

```
from bs4 import BeautifulSoup
```

This line tells Python to import the BeautifulSoup class from the bs4 module, which is the main module of the BeautifulSoup library.

Once you have imported BeautifulSoup, you can start using it to parse HTML and XML files. The most common way to do this is by creating a BeautifulSoup object and passing the HTML or XML content to it. For example, if you have a HTML file called "index.html" that you want to parse, you can do so using the following code:

```
with open("index.html") as file:
soup = BeautifulSoup(file, 'html.parser')
```

This code opens the "index.html" file and creates a BeautifulSoup object called `soup` using the 'html.parser' parser. You can now use the `soup` object to extract data from the HTML file.

One of the main features of BeautifulSoup is its ability to navigate and search through the HTML or XML content. You can use various methods and properties of the BeautifulSoup object to find specific elements, extract text, and manipulate the content as needed. For example, you can use the `find()` method to find the first occurrence of a specific tag in the HTML file:

```
title = soup.find('title') print(title.text)
```

This code finds the first `` tag in the HTML file and prints out the text content of the tag. You can also use the `find_all()` method to find all occurrences of a specific tag in the HTML file:

```
links = soup.find_all('a')
for link in links:
 print(link.get('href'))
```

This code finds all `<a>` tags in the HTML file and prints out the value of the 'href' attribute for each tag.

In addition to navigating and searching through the HTML or XML content, BeautifulSoup also provides methods for modifying the content. You can use the `insert()` method to insert new elements into the HTML file, the `replace_with()` method to replace existing elements, and the `extract()` method to remove elements from the file.

Overall, BeautifulSoup is a powerful and versatile library for web scraping in Python. It provides a simple and intuitive interface for parsing HTML and XML files, navigating and searching through the content, and extracting and manipulating data as needed.

By following the installation and usage instructions outlined in this article, you can start using BeautifulSoup in your Python scripts and take advantage of its capabilities for web scraping.

Parsing and Navigating HTML

Parsing and navigating HTML in any programming language is a crucial skill for web developers. HTML, or Hypertext Markup Language, is the standard language used to create web pages. It consists of various tags and attributes that define the structure and content of a webpage. Parsing and navigating HTML involves extracting information from HTML documents and traversing the DOM (Document Object Model) to manipulate elements on a webpage.

There are several ways to parse and navigate HTML in different programming languages, such as JavaScript, Python, Ruby, and PHP. In this article, we will explore some common techniques and libraries used for parsing and navigating HTML in these languages.

JavaScript is a popular programming language for web development, and it is commonly used to manipulate HTML elements on a webpage. One of the most widely used libraries for parsing and navigating HTML in JavaScript is the DOM API. The DOM API provides a set of methods and properties for accessing and manipulating elements in an HTML document. For example, you can use the getElementById() method to retrieve an element by its ID, or the getElementsByTagName() method to retrieve all elements of a certain tag name.

Another popular library for parsing and navigating HTML in JavaScript is jQuery. jQuery simplifies HTML traversal and manipulation by providing a set of easy-to-use methods and functions. For example, you can use the find() method to select elements that match a specific CSS selector, or the text() method to get or set the text content of an element.

Python is another popular programming language for web development, and it has several libraries for parsing and navigating HTML. One of the most commonly used libraries is BeautifulSoup, which provides a simple and intuitive API for parsing HTML documents. BeautifulSoup allows you to navigate the DOM tree and extract information from HTML elements using methods like find() and find_all().

Another popular library for parsing and navigating HTML in Python is lxml, which is a high-performance XML and HTML parsing library. Lxml provides a more advanced API than BeautifulSoup and allows you to parse HTML documents using XPath expressions.

Ruby is a dynamic programming language commonly used for web development, and it has several libraries for parsing and navigating HTML. One of the most popular libraries is Nokogiri, which provides a powerful API for parsing and navigating XML and HTML documents. Nokogiri allows you to search and manipulate HTML elements using CSS selectors or XPath expressions.

PHP is a server-side scripting language commonly used for web development, and it also has libraries for parsing and navigating HTML. One of the most popular libraries is PHP Simple HTML DOM Parser, which provides a simple and easy-to-use API for parsing HTML documents. PHP Simple HTML DOM Parser allows you to navigate the DOM tree and extract information from HTML elements using methods like find() and find_all().

In conclusion, parsing and navigating HTML in any programming language is a fundamental skill for web developers. By using the right libraries and techniques, you can easily extract information from HTML documents and manipulate elements on a webpage.

Whether you are using JavaScript, Python, Ruby, or PHP, there are libraries available to help you parse and navigate HTML effectively. Mastering these skills will enable you to create dynamic and interactive web applications that provide a seamless user experience.

Extracting Data Efficiently

Extracting data efficiently in any programming language is a crucial skill for data scientists, analysts, and developers. Whether you are working with large datasets, web scraping, or extracting information from databases, having the ability to efficiently extract data can save time and resources. In this article, we will discuss some tips and techniques to help you extract data efficiently in any programming language.

Use the right tools and libraries:

One of the most important factors in extracting data efficiently is using the right tools and libraries. Depending on the type of data you are working with, there are various libraries and tools available in different programming languages that can help you extract data more efficiently. For example, if you are working with web scraping, libraries like BeautifulSoup in Python or Cheerio in Node.js can help you extract data from HTML documents easily. Similarly, if you are working with databases, libraries like SQLAlchemy in Python or JDBC in Java can help you extract data from databases efficiently.

Optimize your queries:

When working with databases or APIs, optimizing your queries can significantly improve the efficiency of data extraction. Make sure to use indexes on columns that are frequently queried, avoid using wildcard characters in your queries, and limit the number of columns retrieved to only those that are necessary. Additionally, batching your queries can help reduce the number of round trips to the database or API, improving the overall performance of data extraction.

Use caching:

Caching is a technique that can help you store and reuse previously extracted data, reducing the need to extract the same data repeatedly. By caching data locally or using a distributed caching system, you can improve the efficiency of data extraction and reduce the load on the data source. However, make sure to invalidate the cache when the data source is updated to ensure that you are always working with the latest data.

Parallelize data extraction:

When working with large datasets or multiple data sources, parallelizing data extraction can help you extract data more efficiently. By running multiple extraction processes concurrently, you can take advantage of multi-core processors and reduce the overall extraction time. However, be mindful of the resources available on your machine and the limitations of the data source to avoid overloading the system.

Monitor and optimize performance:
Monitoring the performance of your data extraction processes is essential to identify bottlenecks and optimize the efficiency of data extraction. Use tools like profilers and performance monitoring tools to identify areas of improvement, such as slow queries or inefficient data processing. By continuously monitoring and optimizing performance, you can ensure that your data extraction processes are running efficiently and smoothly.

In conclusion, extracting data efficiently in any programming language requires a combination of the right tools, techniques, and optimization strategies. By using the right tools and libraries, optimizing your queries, using caching, parallelizing data extraction, and monitoring performance, you can extract data more efficiently and effectively. With these tips and techniques, you can improve the speed and reliability of your data extraction processes, allowing you to work more efficiently with large datasets and complex data sources.

Efficient Data Extraction with Scrapy

Scrapy is a powerful and efficient web crawling and web scraping framework written in Python. It allows users to easily extract data from websites and save it in a structured format, such as JSON, CSV, or XML. With its easy-to-use API and robust features, Scrapy is the go-to tool for data extraction tasks.

Efficient data extraction with Scrapy involves several key components, including setting up a Scrapy project, defining a spider, and using selectors to extract data from web pages. In this article, we will explore these components in detail and provide tips for optimizing data extraction with Scrapy.

Setting up a Scrapy project is the first step in efficient data extraction. To create a new Scrapy project, you can use the `scrapy startproject` command in the terminal. This will create a new directory with the necessary files and folders for your Scrapy project. Inside the project directory, you will find the `spiders` folder, where you can define your spiders.

A spider is a class that defines how to extract data from a website. Each spider in a Scrapy project is responsible for crawling a specific website or set of websites and extracting data according to a set of rules. To define a spider, you need to create a new Python file inside the `spiders` folder and define a class that inherits from `scrapy.Spider`.

Within the spider class, you can define the start URLs, parse method, and item selectors. The start URLs are the initial URLs that the spider will crawl, and the parse method is where you define how to extract data from each web page. Item selectors are used to extract specific data fields from the HTML content of a web page.

Selectors are a powerful feature of Scrapy that allow you to extract data from web pages using CSS or XPath expressions. By using selectors, you can easily target specific elements on a web page and extract the desired data. Scrapy provides a built-in selector API that makes it easy to select and extract data from web pages.

To optimize data extraction with Scrapy, you can follow a few best practices. First, you should use efficient selectors to target specific data fields on a web page. By using precise selectors, you can reduce the amount of HTML content that needs to be processed, which can improve the performance of your spider.

Additionally, you can use Scrapy's built-in features, such as middleware and pipelines, to further optimize data extraction. Middleware allows you to customize the behavior of your spider by adding custom processing logic before or after a request is made. Pipelines allow you to process and save extracted data in a structured format, such as a database or file.

Another tip for efficient data extraction with Scrapy is to use the `scrapy shell` command for testing and debugging your selectors. The scrapy shell is an interactive shell that allows you to test selectors and extract data from web pages in real-time. By using the scrapy shell, you can quickly iterate on your selectors and ensure that they are targeting the correct data fields.

In conclusion, efficient data extraction with Scrapy involves setting up a Scrapy project, defining a spider, and using selectors to extract data from web pages. By following best practices and optimizing your selectors, you can improve the performance of your data extraction tasks and extract data more efficiently. Scrapy is a powerful tool for web crawling and web scraping, and with the right techniques, you can extract data from websites with ease.

Chapter 7: Advanced Google Dorks for OSINT

Google dorks, also known as Google hacking or Google dorking, are search queries that use advanced operators to find information that is not easily accessible through regular searches. These operators can be used to narrow down search results and find specific types of information, making them a valuable tool for open source intelligence (OSINT) gathering.

In this article, we will explore some advanced Google dorks that can be used for OSINT purposes. These dorks can help researchers find information about a wide range of topics, including websites, files, databases, and more. By using these dorks, researchers can uncover valuable information that may not be readily available through traditional search methods.

Site-specific dorks: One of the most basic and useful Google dorks is the site-specific dork. By using the "site:" operator followed by a specific website domain, researchers can search only within that site for specific information. For example, using the query "site:example.com password" would search for any instances of the word "password" on the example.com website.

Filetype dorks: Another useful Google dork is the filetype dork, which allows researchers to search for specific types of files on the internet. By using the "filetype:" operator followed by a file extension, such as pdf, doc, or xls, researchers can find files of a specific type. For example, using the query "filetype:pdf confidential" would search for any PDF files containing the word "confidential."

Intitle dorks: The intitle dork allows researchers to search for specific words or phrases in the title of a webpage. By using the "intitle:" operator followed by a keyword, researchers can find webpages that include that keyword in their title. For example, using the query "intitle:login page" would search for webpages with the word "login" in their title.

Link dorks: The link dork allows researchers to search for webpages that link to a specific URL. By using the "link:" operator followed by a URL, researchers can find webpages that contain a link to that URL. For example, using the query "link:example.com" would search for webpages that link to the example.com website.

Cache dorks: The cache dork allows researchers to view a cached version of a webpage that has been indexed by Google. By using the "cache:" operator followed by a URL, researchers can view a cached version of that webpage. This can be useful for accessing information that may have been removed or changed on the live webpage.

Advanced search operators: In addition to the specific dorks mentioned above, researchers can also use a variety of advanced search operators to narrow down search results. Some useful operators include "OR" to search for multiple keywords, "-" to exclude specific keywords, and "*" as a wildcard for unknown words. Researchers can also use quotation marks to search for exact phrases.

Overall, Google dorks are a powerful tool for OSINT researchers looking to uncover information that may not be easily accessible through traditional search methods. By using advanced operators and search techniques, researchers can find valuable information about websites, files, databases, and more.

It is important to use these dorks responsibly and ethically, following all applicable laws and regulations. With practice and experimentation, researchers can become proficient in using Google dorks for OSINT purposes and uncover valuable information on the internet.

Introduction to Google Dorks

Google Dorks, also known as Google hacking or Google dorking, is a technique used by hackers and cybersecurity professionals to find sensitive information on the internet. By using advanced search operators in Google's search engine, users can uncover vulnerabilities, exposed data, and other information that is not intended to be publicly accessible.

The term "dork" in Google Dorks refers to a person who is socially awkward or inept, but in this context, it refers to a clever or skillful person who is able to manipulate Google's search engine to find valuable information. Google Dorks are essentially search queries that are specifically crafted to find certain types of data, such as passwords, usernames, email addresses, and other sensitive information.

Google Dorks can be used for a variety of purposes, including penetration testing, vulnerability assessment, and information gathering. Hackers use Google Dorks to identify potential targets and gather information that can be used in cyber attacks. On the other hand, cybersecurity professionals use Google Dorks to identify vulnerabilities in their own systems and prevent potential security breaches.

There are several advanced search operators that can be used in Google Dorks to narrow down search results and find specific types of information. Some of the most commonly used operators include:

site: This operator restricts the search results to a specific website or domain. For example, using site:example.com will only return results from the domain example.com.

intitle: This operator searches for specific keywords in the title of a webpage. For example, using intitle:login page will return results that have the keyword "login page" in the title.

filetype: This operator searches for specific file types, such as PDFs, Excel spreadsheets, or Word documents. For example, using filetype:pdf will return results that are PDF files.

inurl: This operator searches for specific keywords in the URL of a webpage. For example, using inurl:admin will return results that have the keyword "admin" in the URL.

By combining these operators with specific keywords,

hackers and cybersecurity professionals can uncover a wealth of information that is not readily visible to the average internet user. This information can include sensitive data, configuration files, login credentials, and other valuable information that can be used in cyber attacks.

It is important to note that Google Dorks should only be used for ethical purposes, such as penetration testing and vulnerability assessment. Using Google Dorks to access unauthorized information or launch cyber attacks is illegal and unethical. It is important to always obtain proper authorization before using Google Dorks to search for sensitive information.

In conclusion, Google Dorks are a powerful tool that can be used to find valuable information on the internet. By using advanced search operators in Google's search engine, users can uncover vulnerabilities, exposed data, and other sensitive information that is not intended to be publicly accessible. However, it is important to use Google Dorks ethically and responsibly to avoid legal consequences and protect the security of systems and data.

Crafting Effective Queries - Google dorks and python

Crafting effective queries using Google dorks and Python can greatly enhance your ability to find specific information online. Google dorks are specific search queries that can be used to find information that is not easily accessible through regular searches. By combining Google dorks with Python, you can automate the process of searching for specific information, saving time and effort.

Google dorks are advanced search operators that can be used to narrow down search results and find specific information. They can be used to search for specific file types, websites, and even specific text within a website. By using Google dorks, you can access information that is not easily accessible through regular searches, making it a powerful tool for researchers, journalists, and anyone looking to find specific information online.

Python is a versatile programming language that can be used to automate tasks and processes. By combining Google dorks with Python, you can create scripts that automate the process of searching for specific information online. This can save you time and effort, allowing you to focus on analyzing the information you find rather than spending hours searching for it.

To craft effective queries using Google dorks and Python, you need to understand how Google dorks work and how to use Python to automate the process of searching for specific information. In this article, we will provide an overview of Google dorks, explain how to use Python to automate the process of searching for specific information, and provide examples of effective queries that can be used to find specific information online.

Google dorks are advanced search operators that can be used to narrow down search results and find specific information. Some common Google dorks include:

site: This operator allows you to search for information on a specific website. For example, site:example.com will only return results from the website example.com.

filetype: This operator allows you to search for specific file types. For example, filetype:pdf will only return results that are PDF files.

intitle: This operator allows you to search for specific text in the title of a webpage. For example, intitle:"Python tutorial" will only return results that have "Python tutorial" in the title.

inurl: This operator allows you to search for specific text in the URL of a webpage. For example, inurl:blog will only return results that have "blog" in the URL.

By combining these operators with specific keywords, you can craft effective queries that will help you find the information you are looking for. For example, if you are looking for Python tutorials on the website example.com, you could use the query site:example.com intitle:"Python tutorial" to narrow down your search results.

Python can be used to automate the process of searching for specific information using Google dorks. By using the requests library in Python, you can send HTTP requests to Google's search engine and parse the results to find the information you are looking for. This allows you to automate the process of searching for specific information, saving time and effort.

To use Python to craft effective queries using Google

dorks, you first need to install the requests library. You can do this by running the following command in your terminal:

pip install requests

Once you have installed the requests library, you can use the following code to send a request to Google's search engine and parse the results:

```python
import requests
from bs4 import BeautifulSoup

def google_search(query):

url = f"https://www.google.com/search?q={query}"
headers = {
"User-Agent": "Mozilla/5.0 (Windows NT 10.0; Win64; x64) AppleWebKit/537.36 (KHTML, like Gecko) Chrome/58.0.3029.110 Safari/537.3"
}
response = requests.get(url, headers=headers)
soup = BeautifulSoup(response.text, "html.parser") results = soup.find_all("div", class_="BVGoNb")
for result in results:
title = result.find("h3").text link = result.find("a")["href"]
print(title, link)

query = "Python tutorial" google_search(query)
```

This code sends a request to Google's search engine with the query "Python tutorial" and parses the results to find the titles and links of the search results. You can customize the query to search for specific information using Google dorks, allowing you to find the information you are looking for quickly and easily.

By combining Google dorks with Python, you can automate the process of searching for specific information online, saving time and effort. This can be especially useful for researchers, journalists, and anyone looking to find specific information quickly. By understanding how Google dorks work and how to use Python to automate the process of searching for specific information, you can craft effective queries that will help you find the information you are looking for.

Finding Personal Information - Google dorks and python

Finding personal information online has become easier than ever with the advent of Google dorks and Python scripts. Google dorks are specific search queries that can be used to find sensitive information that is not easily accessible through regular search methods. Python scripts, on the other hand, can be used to automate the process of searching for personal information online. In this article, we will explore how Google dorks and Python can be used together to find personal information online.

Google dorks are powerful search queries that can be used to find specific types of information on the internet. These queries can be used to search for a wide range of sensitive information, including email addresses, phone numbers, social security numbers, and more. By using Google dorks, it is possible to find personal information that is not easily accessible through regular search methods.

There are many different types of Google dorks that can be used to find personal information online. Some common examples include:

"filetype:pdf" followed by a specific search term: This query can be used to find PDF files that contain the search term. PDF files often contain sensitive information such as resumes, financial documents, and more.

"site:linkedin.com" followed by a specific search term: This query can be used to search for specific information on LinkedIn profiles. LinkedIn profiles often contain personal information such as job history, education, and contact information.

"intitle:contact" followed by a specific search term: This query can be used to find web pages that contain contact information related to the search term. This can include email addresses, phone numbers, and more.

By using Google dorks, it is possible to find a wealth of personal information online. However, manually searching for this information can be time-consuming and inefficient. This is where Python scripts come in.

Python is a versatile programming language that can be used to automate a wide range of tasks, including searching for personal information online. By writing a Python script that uses Google dorks to search for personal information, it is possible to quickly and efficiently gather large amounts of data.

There are many different ways that Python can be used to search for personal information online. One common approach is to use the "requests" library to send HTTP requests to Google's search engine and parse the results. By writing a script that sends a series of requests using different Google dorks, it is possible to find a wide range of personal information online.

Another approach is to use the "selenium" library to automate the process of searching for personal information online. Selenium is a powerful tool that can be used to control web browsers and interact with web pages programmatically. By writing a Python script that uses Selenium to perform Google searches and extract the results, it is possible to find personal information online in a more automated way.

In addition to using Google dorks and Python scripts to find personal information online, there are also other tools and techniques that can be used. For example, there are specialized search engines that are designed to find specific types of personal information, such as email addresses or phone numbers. By using these tools in conjunction with Google dorks and Python scripts, it is possible to find even more personal information online.

It is important to note that finding personal information online using Google dorks and Python scripts can raise ethical and legal concerns. It is important to use these tools responsibly and ethically, and to ensure that any personal information that is found is used in a legal and ethical manner.

In conclusion, Google dorks and Python scripts can be powerful tools for finding personal information online. By using Google dorks to search for specific types of information and writing Python scripts to automate the process, it is possible to quickly and efficiently gather large amounts of personal information. However, it is important to use these tools responsibly and ethically, and to ensure that any personal information that is found is used in a legal and ethical manner.

Chapter 8: Introduction Social Media OSINT

Social media open source intelligence (OSINT) has become an increasingly important tool for gathering information in today's digital age. With the rise of social media platforms such as Facebook, Twitter, Instagram, and LinkedIn, there is a wealth of data available for analysis and research. OSINT refers to the process of collecting and analyzing information from publicly available sources, including social media, to gather intelligence and insights.

The use of social media OSINT has revolutionized the way organizations and individuals gather information. It allows for real-time monitoring of events, trends, and conversations, providing valuable insights into public sentiment, opinions, and behaviors. By analyzing social media data, researchers can identify patterns, trends, and relationships that can help inform decision-making and strategic planning.

One of the key benefits of social media OSINT is its accessibility. Unlike traditional intelligence-gathering methods, which often require specialized training and resources, social media OSINT can be accessed by anyone with an internet connection. This democratization of information has leveled the playing field, allowing individuals and organizations of all sizes to access valuable insights and intelligence.

Social media OSINT is also a valuable tool for law

enforcement and security agencies. By monitoring social media platforms, these organizations can identify potential threats, track criminal activity, and gather evidence for investigations. In some cases, social media OSINT has even been used to prevent crimes before they occur, by identifying individuals who may pose a risk to public safety.

In addition to its applications in security and intelligence, social media OSINT is also used in marketing, business intelligence, and competitive analysis. By monitoring social media conversations and trends, organizations can gain valuable insights into consumer preferences, market trends, and competitor strategies. This information can be used to inform marketing campaigns, product development, and business strategies.

Despite its many benefits, social media OSINT also poses challenges and ethical considerations. The vast amount of data available on social media platforms can be overwhelming, and sorting through it to find relevant information can be time-consuming and labor-intensive. There are also concerns about privacy and data security, as the information gathered through social media OSINT is often personal and sensitive.

To address these challenges, organizations and individuals using social media OSINT must adhere to ethical guidelines and best practices. This includes obtaining consent from individuals before collecting and analyzing their social media data, ensuring that the information gathered is accurate and reliable, and protecting the privacy and security of the data collected.

In conclusion, social media OSINT is a powerful tool for gathering intelligence and insights from publicly available sources. It has revolutionized the way organizations and individuals gather information, providing valuable insights into public sentiment, opinions, and behaviors. While it poses challenges and ethical considerations, when used responsibly, social media OSINT can provide valuable insights that can inform decision-making, strategic planning, and operational activities.

OSINT on Facebook - google dorks python – commands

Open-source intelligence (OSINT) is a valuable tool for gathering information from publicly available sources, and one of the most popular platforms for OSINT is Facebook. By utilizing Google dorks and Python commands, researchers and analysts can extract valuable data from Facebook to uncover insights and trends.

Google dorks are search queries that use advanced operators to find specific information that is not readily accessible through conventional search methods. By using Google dorks, analysts can narrow down their search results to find relevant information on Facebook.

Python is a powerful programming language that can be used to automate tasks and extract data from websites. By using Python commands, analysts can create scripts to scrape Facebook data and analyze it for patterns and trends.

In this article, we will explore how to use Google dorks and Python commands to conduct OSINT on Facebook. We will cover the basics of Google dorks, how to use Python for web scraping, and provide examples of commands that can be used to extract data from Facebook.

Google Dorks for Facebook OSINT

Google dorks can be used to search for specific information on Facebook, such as user profiles, groups, events, and posts. By using advanced operators in Google search, analysts can narrow down their search results to find the information they are looking for.

Here are some examples of Google dorks that can be used for Facebook OSINT:

site:facebook.com "John Doe"

This dork will search for the name "John Doe" on Facebook. By using the site operator, the search results will be limited to Facebook.com.

site:facebook.com inurl:profile.php?id=

This dork will search for user profiles on Facebook. By using the inurl operator, the search results will include URLs that contain "profile.php?id=".

site:facebook.com intitle:events

This dork will search for events on Facebook. By using the intitle operator, the search results will include pages that have "events" in the title.

site:facebook.com intitle:groups

This dork will search for groups on Facebook. By using the intitle operator, the search results will include pages that have "groups" in the title.

site:facebook.com intext:password

This dork will search for posts or pages on Facebook that contain the word "password". By using the intext operator, the search results will include pages that have the word "password" in the text.

Using Google dorks, analysts can quickly find relevant information on Facebook and gather data for further analysis.

Python Commands for Facebook OSINT

Python is a versatile programming language that can be used for web scraping, data analysis, and automation. By using Python commands, analysts can create scripts to extract data from Facebook and analyze it for patterns and trends.

Here are some Python commands that can be used for Facebook OSINT:

Importing the necessary libraries:
```
import requests
from bs4 import BeautifulSoup
```

Sending a request to Facebook:

```
url = "https://www.facebook.com" response =
requests.get(url)
soup = BeautifulSoup(response.content, "html.parser")
```

Extracting user profiles:

```
profiles = soup.find_all("a", class_="profile") for profile in
profiles:
print(profile.get("href"))
```

Extracting group names:

```
groups = soup.find_all("div", class_="group") for group in
groups:
print(group.text)
```

Extracting event details:

```
events = soup.find_all("div", class_="event") for event in
events:
print(event.text)
```

By using Python commands, analysts can automate the process of extracting data from Facebook and analyze it for patterns and trends.

Conclusion

In conclusion, OSINT on Facebook can be conducted using Google dorks and Python commands to extract valuable data from the platform. By utilizing advanced search operators in Google dorks, analysts can narrow down their search results to find specific information on Facebook.

Python commands can be used to automate the process of extracting data from Facebook and analyze it for patterns and trends. By combining Google dorks and Python commands, researchers and analysts can uncover valuable insights and trends from Facebook data.

Overall, OSINT on Facebook is a powerful tool for gathering information from publicly available sources and can provide valuable insights for researchers and analysts. By using Google dorks and Python commands, analysts can extract data from Facebook to uncover valuable insights and trends.

OSINT on Twitter - google dorks python advanceds

Open Source Intelligence (OSINT) is a valuable tool for gathering information from publicly available sources, and Twitter is one of the most popular platforms for conducting OSINT investigations. By using advanced Google dorks and Python scripting, researchers can enhance their ability to extract valuable data and insights from the vast amount of information available on Twitter.

Google dorks are specialized search queries that can be used to find specific types of information on the internet. By combining Google dorks with Python scripting, researchers can automate the process of searching for and analyzing data on Twitter, allowing them to uncover valuable insights more efficiently.

In this article, we will explore how to use advanced Google

dorks and Python scripting to conduct OSINT investigations on Twitter. We will cover the basics of Google dorks, how to use them to search for information on Twitter, and how to automate the process using Python scripting.

Understanding Google Dorks

Google dorks are specialized search queries that can be used to find specific types of information on the internet. By using advanced operators and search syntax, researchers can narrow down their search results and find the information they are looking for more efficiently.

Some common Google dorks that can be used to search for information on Twitter include:

site:twitter.com [keyword]: This search query allows you to search for tweets containing a specific keyword on Twitter.

inurl:twitter.com [keyword]: This search query allows you to search for tweets containing a specific keyword in the URL on Twitter.

intitle:twitter.com [keyword]: This search query allows you to search for tweets containing a specific keyword in the title on Twitter.

By combining these search queries with other operators, researchers can narrow down their search results and find the information they are looking for more efficiently.

Using Google Dorks to Search for Information on Twitter

To use Google dorks to search for information on Twitter, researchers can simply enter the search query into the Google search bar and review the search results. By analyzing the search results, researchers can uncover valuable insights and information about a specific topic, individual, or organization.

For example, researchers can use the following Google dork to search for tweets containing a specific keyword on Twitter:

site:twitter.com [keyword]

By entering this search query into the Google search bar, researchers can find tweets containing the specified keyword on Twitter. They can then review the search results to uncover valuable insights and information about the topic.

Automating the Process with Python Scripting

While Google dorks can be a valuable tool for conducting OSINT investigations on Twitter, researchers can enhance their capabilities by automating the process using Python scripting. By writing Python scripts that interact with the Twitter API, researchers can extract, analyze, and visualize data from Twitter more efficiently.

To get started with Python scripting for OSINT on Twitter, researchers can follow these steps:

Install the Tweepy Library: Tweepy is a Python library that provides easy-to-use access to the Twitter API. Researchers can install the Tweepy library by running the following command in the terminal:

pip install tweepy

Create a Twitter Developer Account: To access the Twitter API, researchers need to create a Twitter developer account and obtain API keys. They can do this by visiting the Twitter Developer Portal and creating a new application.

Write Python Scripts: Researchers can write Python scripts that interact with the Twitter API using the Tweepy library. They can use the API keys obtained from their Twitter developer account to authenticate their requests and access Twitter data.

Extract and Analyze Data: Researchers can use Python scripts to extract data from Twitter, analyze it, and visualize the results. They can search for tweets containing specific keywords, analyze user profiles, and track trends over time.

By automating the process with Python scripting, researchers can enhance their ability to extract valuable insights and information from Twitter more efficiently.

Conclusion

In conclusion, advanced Google dorks and Python scripting can be valuable tools for conducting OSINT investigations on Twitter. By using specialized search queries and scripting techniques, researchers can extract, analyze, and visualize data from Twitter more efficiently, allowing them to uncover valuable insights and information about a wide range of topics, individuals, and organizations.

By combining Google dorks with Python scripting, researchers can enhance their capabilities and conduct more thorough and effective OSINT investigations on Twitter. By following the steps outlined in this article, researchers can get started with advanced OSINT techniques and unlock the full potential of Twitter as a valuable source of information.

OSINT on LinkedIn - google dorks - python examples

Open Source Intelligence (OSINT) is a valuable tool for gathering information from publicly available sources, and one platform that is rich in potential data is LinkedIn. With over 700 million users worldwide, LinkedIn is a goldmine of professional information that can be leveraged for various purposes, such as research, recruitment, competitive analysis, and more.

One way to gather information from LinkedIn is by using Google dorks, which are specialized search queries that can help you find specific types of information on the web. By combining Google dorks with Python scripting, you can automate the process of collecting data from LinkedIn profiles, making it faster and more efficient.

In this article, we will explore how to use Google dorks and Python to conduct OSINT on LinkedIn. We will provide examples of Google dorks that can be used to find specific types of information on LinkedIn, as well as Python scripts that can be used to automate the process of collecting data from LinkedIn profiles.

Google Dorks for LinkedIn OSINT

Google dorks are search queries that are used to find specific types of information on the web. By using Google dorks, you can narrow down your search results to find exactly what you are looking for. Here are some Google dorks that can be used to find information on LinkedIn:

site:linkedin.com/in "keyword" - This dork can be used to find LinkedIn profiles that contain a specific keyword in their URL. For example, if you are looking for profiles related to cybersecurity, you can use the dork site:linkedin.com/in cybersecurity to find relevant profiles.

site:linkedin.com/pub "keyword" - This dork can be used to find LinkedIn profiles that contain a specific keyword in their public profile. For example, if you are looking for profiles related to data science, you can use the dork site:linkedin.com/pub data science to find relevant profiles.

site:linkedin.com "company name" - This dork can be used to find LinkedIn profiles that are associated with a specific company. For example, if you are looking for profiles of employees at Google, you can use the dork site:linkedin.com Google to find relevant profiles.

site:linkedin.com "location" - This dork can be used to find LinkedIn profiles that are located in a specific geographic location. For example, if you are looking for profiles of professionals in New York City, you can use the dork site:linkedin.com New York City to find relevant profiles.

These are just a few examples of Google dorks that can be used to find information on LinkedIn. By combining these dorks with Python scripting, you can automate the process of collecting data from LinkedIn profiles.

Python Examples for LinkedIn OSINT

Python is a powerful programming language that can be used to automate various tasks, including data collection from websites. By using Python, you can write scripts that can scrape data from LinkedIn profiles and save it in a structured format for further analysis. Here are some Python examples that can be used for LinkedIn OSINT:

Using the requests library to scrape LinkedIn profiles:

import requests

url = 'https://www.linkedin.com/in/johndoe' response = requests.get(url) print(response.text)

This script uses the requests library to send a GET request to a LinkedIn profile URL and prints the HTML content of the response. You can then use BeautifulSoup or another parsing library to extract specific information from the HTML content.

Using the BeautifulSoup library to parse LinkedIn profiles:

```
from bs4 import BeautifulSoup
import requests

url = 'https://www.linkedin.com/in/johndoe' response = requests.get(url)
soup = BeautifulSoup(response.text, 'html.parser')

name = soup.find('h1', {'class': 'pv-top-card-section name'}).text headline = soup.find('p', {'class': 'pv-top-card-section_headline'}).text

print('Name:', name) print('Headline:', headline)
```

This script uses BeautifulSoup to parse the HTML content of a LinkedIn profile and extract the name and headline of the profile. You can modify the script to extract other information, such as work experience, education, skills, and more.

Automating the collection of LinkedIn profiles using Google dorks: import requests from bs4 import BeautifulSoup

```
keywords = ['cybersecurity', 'data science', 'machine learning'] results = []

for keyword in keywords:

url = f'https://www.google.com/search?q=site:linkedin.com/in
```

```
{keyword}' response = requests.get(url)
soup = BeautifulSoup(response.text, 'html.parser') profiles
= soup.find_all('div', {'class': 'r'})
for profile in profiles:

link = profile.find('a')['href'] results.append(link)

print(results)
```

This script automates the process of collecting LinkedIn profile URLs using Google dorks.

Chapter 9: Extracting Data from Social Media APIs

Social media platforms have become an integral part of our daily lives, with millions of users sharing their thoughts, photos, and videos every day. These platforms provide a wealth of data that can be analyzed to gain insights into user behavior, preferences, and trends. One way to access this data is through social media APIs, which allow developers to interact with the platform and extract information programmatically.

There are several popular social media APIs available, including those for platforms like Facebook, Twitter, Instagram, and LinkedIn. These APIs provide a wide range of functionalities, such as retrieving user profiles, posts, comments, likes, and more. By leveraging these APIs, developers can access a wealth of data that can be used for various purposes, such as social media monitoring, sentiment analysis, trend analysis, and personalized recommendations.

To extract data from social media APIs, developers first need to register for an API key, which is a unique identifier that allows them to access the platform's data. The process of obtaining an API key varies depending on the platform, but typically involves creating a developer account, agreeing to the platform's terms of service, and generating a key that will be used to authenticate API requests.

Once developers have obtained an API key, they can start

making API requests to retrieve data from the platform. These requests are typically made using HTTP protocols, such as GET, POST, PUT, and DELETE, and can be sent to specific endpoints that correspond to different functionalities offered by the API. For example, to retrieve a user's profile information from Twitter, developers can make a GET request to the
/users/show endpoint, passing the user's username as a parameter.

In addition to retrieving data, social media APIs also allow developers to interact with the platform by performing actions such as posting tweets, liking posts, following users, and sending messages. These actions can be performed by making POST requests to the corresponding endpoints, along with the necessary parameters required for the action.

One of the key benefits of using social media APIs is the ability to access real-time data from the platform. This means that developers can retrieve the latest posts, comments, and likes as soon as they are published, allowing them to monitor trends and user interactions in real-time. This real-time data can be invaluable for businesses looking to stay ahead of the competition and engage with their audience in a timely manner.

Another benefit of using social media APIs is the ability to access a wide range of data points that can be used for analysis. For example, developers can retrieve user demographics, interests, engagement metrics, and more, which can be used to create detailed user profiles and segment users based on their behavior. This data can then be used to personalize content, target ads, and optimize marketing campaigns for better results.

In addition to accessing data from social media APIs, developers can also use these APIs to integrate social media features into their own applications. For example, developers can allow users to sign in with their social media accounts, share content on social media platforms, and display social media feeds within their app. By leveraging social media APIs, developers can enhance the user experience and increase engagement with their app.

When working with social media APIs, developers need to be mindful of the platform's rate limits, which restrict the number of API requests that can be made within a certain time frame. Exceeding these rate limits can result in temporary or permanent suspension of API access, so developers need to carefully manage their API usage to avoid any disruptions.

In conclusion, extracting data from social media APIs is a powerful tool for gaining insights into user behavior, preferences, and trends. By leveraging these APIs, developers can access a wealth of data that can be used for various purposes, such as social media monitoring, sentiment analysis, trend analysis, and personalized recommendations. With the right approach and careful management of API usage, developers can harness the power of social media APIs to enhance their applications and drive better results.

Accessing Social Media APIs – python

Social media platforms have become an integral part of our daily lives, allowing us to connect with friends, family, and even strangers from all around the world. With the rise of social media, there has also been a growing demand for developers to access social media APIs in order to create innovative applications and services that interact with these platforms.

One popular programming language that is commonly used to access social media APIs is Python. Python is a versatile and powerful language that is known for its simplicity and readability, making it an ideal choice for developers looking to integrate social media functionality into their applications.

In this article, we will explore how to access social media APIs using Python, including how to authenticate with the API, make requests, and handle responses. We will also discuss some best practices for working with social media APIs and provide examples of how to access popular social media platforms such as Facebook, Twitter, and Instagram.

Authentication

One of the first steps in accessing a social media API is to authenticate with the platform. Most social media APIs require developers to obtain an access token or API key in order to make requests to the API. This token is used to verify the identity of the developer and ensure that they have permission to access the API.

To authenticate with a social media API in Python,

developers can use the requests library to make HTTP requests to the API. The requests library is a popular HTTP library for Python that simplifies the process of making HTTP requests and handling responses.

Here is an example of how to authenticate with the Twitter API using the requests library: import requests
# Set up authentication credentials consumer_key = 'your_consumer_key'   consumer_secret   = 'your_consumer_secret'   access_token   = 'your_access_token'
access_token_secret = 'your_access_token_secret'

Create an OAuth1 session session = requests.Session()
session.auth   =   (consumer_key,   consumer_secret)
session.headers   =   {'Authorization':   f'Bearer {access_token}'}

Make a request to the Twitter API
response   =
session.get('https://api.twitter.com/1.1/account/verify_cre dentials.json')

Print the response print(response.json())

In this example, we set up authentication credentials for the Twitter API, including the consumer key, consumer secret, access token, and access token secret. We then create an OAuth1 session using the requests library and make a request to the Twitter API to verify the credentials of the authenticated user.

Making Requests

Once authenticated, developers can start making requests to the social media API to retrieve data or perform actions on behalf of the authenticated user. Social media APIs typically provide a range of endpoints that developers can use to interact with the platform, such as retrieving user information, posting updates, and searching for content.

To make a request to a social media API in Python, developers can use the requests library to send HTTP requests to the API endpoint. The requests library supports various HTTP methods, such as GET, POST, PUT, and DELETE, which can be used to interact with the API.

Here is an example of how to make a request to the Facebook Graph API using the requests library: import requests
Set up authentication credentials access_token = 'your_access_token'

# Make a request to the Facebook Graph API
response = requests.get(f'https://graph.facebook.com/me?fields=id,name&access_token={access_token}')

Print the response print(response.json())

In this example, we set up authentication credentials for the Facebook Graph API using an access token. We then make a GET request to the API endpoint 'https://graph.facebook.com/me' to retrieve the user's ID and name. The response from the API is printed to the console using the json() method.

Handling Responses

After making a request to a social media API, developers will receive a response from the API that contains the requested data or information. The response from the API is typically in JSON format, which can be parsed and manipulated using Python's built-in JSON library.

To handle responses from a social media API in Python, developers can use the json() method provided by the requests library to convert the response into a Python dictionary. This allows developers to easily access and extract data from the response for further processing.

Here is an example of how to handle a response from the Twitter API using the requests library: import requests
Set up authentication credentials

```
consumer_key = 'your_consumer_key' consumer_secret
=       'your_consumer_secret'       access_token    =
'your_access_token'         access_token_secret        =
'your_access_token_secret'
```

```
# Create an OAuth1 session session = requests.Session()
session.auth   =   (consumer_key,   consumer_secret)
session.headers      =      {'Authorization':      f'Bearer
{access_token}'}
```

```
# Make a request to the Twitter API
response                                                  =
session.get('https://api.twitter.com/1.1/account/verify_cre
```

dentials.json')

Parse the response data = response.json()

Extract user information from the response user_id =
data['id']
user_name = data['

Collecting Data from Twitter API – python

Collecting data from Twitter API using Python is a
powerful way to extract valuable insights from one of the
most popular social media platforms in the world. With
over 330 million monthly active users, Twitter is a
treasure trove of information that can be used for various
purposes such as sentiment analysis, trend analysis,
customer feedback, and more.

In this article, we will explore how to collect data from
Twitter API using Python. We will cover the basics of
setting up a Twitter developer account, creating a Twitter
API application, and using Python libraries such as
Tweepy to interact with the Twitter API.

Setting up a Twitter Developer Account

Before we can start collecting data from Twitter API, we
need to set up a Twitter developer account. To do this,
follow these steps:

Go to the Twitter Developer website at
https://developer.twitter.com/en.
Click on the "Apply" button to create a developer account.

Fill out the required information and agree to the terms and conditions.

Once your account is approved, create a new Twitter application by clicking on the "Create an app" button.

Fill out the application details such as the name, description, website, and use case.

After creating the application, navigate to the "Keys and tokens" tab to generate the necessary API keys and access tokens.

Creating a Twitter API Application

To collect data from Twitter API using Python, we need to create a Twitter API application. This application will allow us to authenticate and interact with the Twitter API endpoints. Follow these steps to create a Twitter API application:

Log in to your Twitter developer account.

Go to the "Projects & Apps" tab and click on the "Create App" button.

Fill out the application details such as the name, description, and use case.

Once the application is created, navigate to the "Keys and tokens" tab to generate the necessary API keys and access tokens.

Copy the consumer key, consumer secret, access token, and access token secret, as we will need them to authenticate our Python script.

Using Tweepy to Interact with Twitter API

Tweepy is a popular Python library that provides an easy-to-use interface for interacting with the Twitter API. To install Tweepy, run the following command in your terminal:

```bash
pip install tweepy
```

Once Tweepy is installed, we can start collecting data from Twitter API using the following steps:

Import the Tweepy library and authenticate with the Twitter API using the API keys and access tokens generated earlier.

```python
import tweepy

consumer_key        =        'YOUR_CONSUMER_KEY'
consumer_secret     =     'YOUR_CONSUMER_SECRET'
access_token        =        'YOUR_ACCESS_TOKEN'
access_token_secret                            =
'YOUR_ACCESS_TOKEN_SECRET'

auth      =      tweepy.OAuthHandler(consumer_key,
consumer_secret) auth.set_access_token(access_token,
access_token_secret)

api = tweepy.API(auth)
```

Use the Tweepy API object to interact with the Twitter API

endpoints. For example, we can search for tweets containing a specific keyword using the `search` method.

```python
tweets = api.search(q='Python', count=10)

for tweet in tweets:
print(tweet.text)
```

Collecting data from Twitter API can be done in various ways such as searching for tweets, fetching user timelines, streaming real-time tweets, and more. The possibilities are endless when it comes to collecting data from Twitter API using Python.

Remember to handle rate limits and errors when interacting with the Twitter API to avoid getting blocked or banned. Tweepy provides built-in methods for handling rate limits and errors, so make sure to implement them in your Python script.

Conclusion

Collecting data from Twitter API using Python is a powerful way to extract valuable insights from one of the most popular social media platforms in the world. By setting up a Twitter developer account, creating a Twitter API application, and using Python libraries such as Tweepy, we can easily interact with the Twitter API endpoints and collect data for various purposes such as sentiment analysis, trend analysis, customer feedback, and more.

In this article, we covered the basics of collecting data from Twitter API using Python. We learned how to set up a Twitter developer account, create a Twitter API application, and use Tweepy to interact with the Twitter API.

With the knowledge gained from this article, you can now start collecting data from Twitter API and unlock the full potential of Twitter data for your projects.

Collecting Data from Facebook Graph API – python

Collecting data from Facebook Graph API using Python can be a powerful tool for businesses and developers looking to gather insights and information from the world's largest social media platform. The Facebook Graph API allows users to access and retrieve data from Facebook's vast database, including user profiles, posts, comments, likes, and more. In this article, we will explore how to collect data from Facebook Graph API using Python and how to use this data to gain valuable insights.

To get started with collecting data from Facebook Graph API, you will first need to create a Facebook App and obtain an access token. This access token is required to make requests to the API and access data from Facebook's platform. You can create a new Facebook App by visiting the Facebook Developer website and following the instructions to create a new app. Once you have created your app, you will need to obtain an access token by following the authentication process outlined in the Facebook Developer documentation.

Once you have obtained your access token, you can start making requests to the Facebook Graph API using Python. To do this, you will need to install the `requests` library in Python, which allows you to make HTTP requests to the API. You can install the `requests` library using `pip` by running the following command in your terminal:

```
pip install requests
```

Once you have installed the `requests` library, you can start making requests to the Facebook Graph API. To make a request to the API, you will need to specify the endpoint you want to access and include your access token in the request headers. For example, to retrieve information about a specific user, you can make a request to the `/me` endpoint using the following code:

```python
import requests

access_token = 'your_access_token'
url = 'https://graph.facebook.com/v12.0/me'

headers = {
'Authorization': f'Bearer {access_token}'
}

response = requests.get(url, headers=headers) data = response.json()
```

```
print(data)
```

This code snippet makes a GET request to the `/me` endpoint of the Facebook Graph API and retrieves information about the currently authenticated user. The response from the API is stored in the `data` variable and printed to the console. You can modify this code to make requests to other endpoints and retrieve different types of data from Facebook's platform.

In addition to retrieving user information, you can also collect data about posts, comments, likes, and other interactions on Facebook using the Graph API. For example, you can retrieve a user's posts by making a request to the `/me/posts` endpoint:

```python
url = 'https://graph.facebook.com/v12.0/me/posts'

response = requests.get(url, headers=headers) data = response.json()

print(data)
```

This code snippet retrieves the posts made by the currently authenticated user from Facebook's platform. You can modify this code to retrieve posts from other users or pages by changing the endpoint in the request.

In addition to retrieving data from Facebook Graph API,

you can also analyze and process this data to gain insights and information. For example, you can use Python libraries such as `pandas` and `matplotlib` to analyze and visualize the data retrieved from the API. You can use `pandas` to manipulate and process the data, and `matplotlib` to create visualizations such as charts and graphs.

For example, you can use `pandas` to create a DataFrame from the data retrieved from the Facebook Graph API and analyze the posts made by a user. You can then use `matplotlib` to create a bar chart showing the number of likes and comments on each post:

```python
import pandas as pd
import matplotlib.pyplot as plt

posts = data['data']
df = pd.DataFrame(posts)

df['likes_count'] = df['likes'].apply(lambda x: len(x['data'])) df['comments_count'] = df['comments'].apply(lambda x: len(x['data']))

plt.bar(df['id'], df['likes_count'], label='Likes')
plt.bar(df['id'], df['comments_count'], label='Comments')

plt.xlabel('Post ID') plt.ylabel('Count') plt.legend()

plt.show()
```

This code snippet creates a DataFrame from the posts retrieved from the Facebook Graph API and calculates the number of likes and comments on each post. It then creates a bar chart showing the number of likes and comments on each post. You can modify this code to analyze other types of data retrieved from the API and create different visualizations.

In conclusion, collecting data from Facebook Graph API using Python can be a valuable tool for businesses and developers looking to gather insights and information from the world's largest social media platform. By making requests to the API, retrieving data, and analyzing this data using Python libraries, you can gain valuable insights and information that can help you make informed decisions and improve your business or application. With the right tools and techniques, you can harness the power of Facebook's

Chapter 10: Email and Phone OSINT

Email and Phone OSINT, or Open Source Intelligence, is a valuable tool for gathering information about individuals or organizations using publicly available data from online sources. By utilizing Email and Phone OSINT techniques, investigators can uncover a wealth of information that can be used for various purposes, such as conducting background checks, verifying identities, or investigating potential threats.

One of the key benefits of Email and Phone OSINT is its ability to provide a comprehensive view of an individual or organization by aggregating data from multiple sources. This can include social media profiles, public records, online directories, and other online platforms where individuals may have a presence. By analyzing this data, investigators can piece together a detailed profile that can help them better understand the subject of their investigation.

When conducting Email and Phone OSINT, it is important to use a variety of tools and techniques to gather as much information as possible. This can include using search engines to look up email addresses or phone numbers, using social media platforms to find profiles associated with the subject, and using online directories to search for contact information. By casting a wide net and exploring multiple sources, investigators can increase the likelihood of finding relevant information.

In addition to gathering information, Email and Phone

OSINT can also be used to verify the accuracy of the data that is already known. For example, if an individual claims to work for a certain company or live in a specific location, investigators can use OSINT techniques to confirm this information by cross-referencing it with publicly available data. This can help to ensure that the information being used is accurate and up-to-date.

Furthermore, Email and Phone OSINT can be used to identify potential risks or threats. By analyzing the online presence of an individual or organization, investigators can uncover any red flags or concerning behavior that may indicate a potential threat. This can include identifying individuals with criminal records, uncovering fraudulent activity, or identifying individuals who may be involved in illegal or unethical behavior.

Overall, Email and Phone OSINT is a powerful tool that can provide valuable insights and information for investigators. By utilizing a variety of tools and techniques, investigators can gather a wealth of information that can help them better understand their subjects and make informed decisions. Whether conducting background checks, verifying identities, or investigating potential threats, Email and Phone OSINT can be a valuable resource for gathering information and conducting investigations.

Techniques for Email Harvesting – python

Email harvesting is the process of collecting email addresses from various sources for the purpose of building email lists or conducting email marketing campaigns. This practice is commonly used by businesses and marketers to reach out to potential customers and promote their products or services. There are various techniques and tools available for email harvesting, and one popular method is using Python programming language.

Python is a versatile and powerful programming language that is widely used in data analysis, web development, and automation. It provides a rich set of libraries and tools that make it easy to automate tasks like email harvesting. In this article, we will discuss some techniques for email harvesting using Python.

Web scraping:
Web scraping is a technique used to extract data from websites. Python provides several libraries like BeautifulSoup and Scrapy that make it easy to scrape websites and extract email addresses. You can write a Python script that scrapes a website for email addresses and saves them to a file or database.

Here is an example of how you can scrape email addresses from a website using BeautifulSoup:

```
```

```
from bs4 import BeautifulSoup import requests

url = 'https://example.com' response = requests.get(url)
```

```python
soup = BeautifulSoup(response.text, 'html.parser')

emails = []
for link in soup.find_all('a'):
if link.get('href') and 'mailto:' in link.get('href'):
email        =       link.get('href').replace('mailto:',       '')
emails.append(email)

print(emails)
```

Email validation:
Before harvesting email addresses, it is important to validate them to ensure that they are valid and deliverable. Python provides libraries like validate_email that can be used to validate email addresses. You can use this library to check if an email address is valid before adding it to your email list.

Here is an example of how you can validate email addresses using the validate_email library:

```
from validate_email_address import validate_email email = 'example@example.com'
```

```
is_valid = validate_email(email) if is_valid:
print('Email address is valid') else:
print('Email address is invalid')
```

Using APIs:
Some websites and services provide APIs that allow you to access their data, including email addresses. You can use Python to interact with these APIs and retrieve email addresses. For example, you can use the Google Maps API to search for businesses and extract their email addresses.

Here is an example of how you can use the Google Maps API to extract email addresses of businesses:

```
import requests

api_key = 'your_api_key' search_query = 'restaurants near me'
url                                                    =
f'https://maps.googleapis.com/maps/api/place/textsearch/json?query={search_query}&key={api_key}'

response = requests.get(url) data = response.json()

emails = []
for result in data['results']:
if 'email' in result:
email = result['email'] emails.append(email)

print(emails)
```

Using email scraping tools:
There are several email scraping tools available that can automate the process of email harvesting. These tools use advanced algorithms to search for email addresses on websites and social media platforms. You can use Python to interact with these tools and extract email addresses.

Here is an example of how you can use the EmailScraper tool to extract email addresses from a website:

```
```

from email_scraper import scrape_emails

url = 'https://example.com' emails = scrape_emails(url)

print(emails)

```
```

Using regular expressions:

Regular expressions are a powerful tool for pattern matching and text processing. You can use regular expressions in Python to search for email addresses in text documents or web pages. By defining a regular expression pattern for email addresses, you can extract email addresses from any text.

Here is an example of how you can use regular expressions to extract email addresses from a text document:

```
```

```
import re

text = 'Contact us at example@example.com or visit our
website at www.example.com' pattern = r'[\w\.-]+@[\w\.-
]+'
emails = re.findall(pattern, text)

print(emails)
```

In conclusion, email harvesting is a common practice used by businesses and marketers to build email lists and conduct email marketing campaigns. Python provides a variety of techniques and tools that make it easy to harvest email addresses from websites, APIs, and text documents. By using Python programming language, you can automate the process of email harvesting and reach out to potential customers effectively.

Validating and Verifying Emails – python

Validating and verifying emails in Python is an essential task for any developer or data analyst working with email data. Ensuring that the email addresses in your database are accurate and valid can help improve the deliverability of your emails and reduce the likelihood of bouncing or being marked as spam. In this article, we will explore different methods and libraries that can be used to validate and verify emails in Python.

Regular Expressions:
One of the simplest ways to validate an email address in Python is to use regular expressions. Regular expressions

are a powerful tool for pattern matching and can be used to define the structure of an email address. Here is an example of a regular expression that can be used to validate an email address:

```python
import re

def validate_email(email):
    pattern = r'^[a-zA-Z0-9_.+-]+@[a-zA-Z0-9-]+\.[a-zA-Z0-9-.]+$'
    return re.match(pattern, email) is not None
```

In this example, the `validate_email` function takes an email address as input and uses a regular expression to check if it matches the expected structure of an email address. If the email address matches the pattern, the function returns `True`, indicating that the email address is valid.

Using the validate_email library:
Another option for validating email addresses in Python is to use the `validate_email` library. This library provides a simple interface for validating email addresses and checking if they are deliverable. Here is an example of how to use the `validate_email` library:

```python
from validate_email_address import validate_email

email = 'example@email.com'
is_valid = validate_email(email)

if is_valid:
```

```
print('The email address is valid') else:
print('The email address is not valid')
```

In this example, the `validate_email` function from the `validate_email_address` library is used to check if the email address is valid. If the email address is valid, the function returns `True`, otherwise it returns `False`.

Verifying email addresses with the py3dns library:
In addition to validating email addresses, it is also important to verify that they are deliverable and can receive emails. The `py3dns` library can be used to check if an email address has a valid domain and can receive emails.

Here is an example of how to use the `py3dns` library to verify an email address:

```python
import py3dns

email = 'example@email.com'
is_valid = py3dns.verify_email_address(email)

if is_valid:
print('The email address is deliverable') else:
print('The email address is not deliverable')
```

In this example, the `verify_email_address` function from the `py3dns` library is used to check if the email address is deliverable. If the email address is deliverable, the function returns `True`, otherwise it returns `False`.

Using the mailboxlayer API:
Another option for verifying email addresses in Python is to use the mailboxlayer API. The mailboxlayer API provides a simple interface for validating email addresses and checking if they are deliverable. Here is an example of how to use the mailboxlayer API to verify an email address:

```python
import requests

api_key = 'YOUR_API_KEY' email = 'example@email.com'

url = f'https://apilayer.com/mailboxlayer?access_key={api_key}&email={email}' response = requests.get(url)
data = response.json()

if data['format_valid'] and data['mx_found']:
print('The email address is deliverable') else:
print('The email address is not deliverable')
```

In this example, a request is made to the mailboxlayer API with the email address to be verified. The response from the API is then checked to see if the email address is deliverable. If the email address is deliverable, the `format_valid` and `mx_found` fields in the response will be `True`.

Conclusion:

Validating and verifying email addresses in Python is an important task that can help improve the quality of your email data and ensure that your emails are delivered successfully. In this article, we have explored different methods and libraries that can be used to validate and verify email addresses in Python, including regular expressions, the `validate_email` library, the `py3dns` library, and the mailboxlayer API. By incorporating these techniques into your data processing pipeline, you can ensure that your email data is accurate and reliable.

Tracking Phone Numbers – python

Tracking phone numbers can be a useful tool for businesses and individuals alike. Whether you are looking to monitor incoming calls for marketing purposes or simply want to keep track of who is contacting you, there are a variety of ways to track phone numbers using Python.

Python is a versatile programming language that is known for its simplicity and ease of use. With its extensive library of modules and packages, Python can be a powerful tool for tracking phone numbers. In this article, we will explore some of the ways in which Python can be used to track phone numbers and monitor incoming calls.

One of the most common ways to track phone numbers using Python is through the use of a phone number lookup service. There are several online services that allow you to input a phone number and receive information about the owner of that number. By using Python to automate this process, you can quickly gather information about incoming calls and track phone numbers in real-time.

To get started, you will need to install the requests module in Python, which will allow you to make HTTP requests to the phone number lookup service. You can do this by running the following command in your terminal:

```python
pip install requests
```

Once you have installed the requests module, you can create a Python script to make a request to the phone number lookup service. Here is an example script that uses the Numverify API to lookup information about a phone number:

```python
import requests

phone_number = input("Enter the phone number you want to lookup: ")
url = f"https://apilayer.com/numverify?access_key=YOUR_ACCESS_KEY&number={phone_number}" response = requests.get(url)
data = response.json()

print("Phone Number: ", data['number']) print("Country Code: ", data['country_code']) print("Country Name: ", data['country_name']) print("Location: ", data['location'])
print("Carrier: ", data['carrier'])
```

In this script, we are using the Numverify API to lookup information about a phone number. You will need to sign up for an access key on the Numverify website in order to use their API. Once you have obtained your access key, you can replace `YOUR_ACCESS_KEY` in the URL with your actual access key.

When you run this script and enter a phone number, it will make a request to the Numverify API and print out information about the phone number, such as the country code, country name, location, and carrier. This can be a useful tool for tracking phone numbers and gathering information about incoming calls.

Another way to track phone numbers using Python is by analyzing call logs from your phone or VoIP service. Many phone systems and VoIP providers offer call detail records that contain information about incoming and outgoing calls, including the phone number, date, and time of the call. By parsing these call logs with Python, you can track phone numbers and analyze call patterns over time.

To get started, you will need to export your call logs from your phone system or VoIP provider in a format that can be read by Python. This may involve exporting the call logs to a CSV file or using an API to retrieve the call logs programmatically. Once you have your call logs in a format that can be read by Python, you can create a script to analyze the data.

Here is an example script that reads a CSV file containing call logs and tracks the frequency of incoming calls from each phone number:

```python
import csv

call_logs = []

with open('call_logs.csv', 'r') as file:
    reader = csv.reader(file)
    for row in reader:
        call_logs.append(row)
phone_numbers = {}
for call in call_logs:
    if call[1] == 'incoming':
        phone_number = call[2]
        if phone_number in phone_numbers:
            phone_numbers[phone_number] += 1
        else:
            phone_numbers[phone_number] = 1

for phone_number, count in phone_numbers.items():
    print(f"Phone Number: {phone_number}, Incoming Calls: {count}")
```

In this script, we are reading a CSV file containing call logs and tracking the frequency of incoming calls from each phone number. The script creates a dictionary called `phone_numbers` to store the count of incoming calls for each phone number, and then prints out the phone number and the number of incoming calls for each phone number.

This can be a useful tool for businesses that want to track the frequency of incoming calls from different phone numbers, or individuals who want to monitor who is contacting them and how often. By analyzing call logs with

Python, you can gain valuable insights into call patterns and identify any suspicious or unwanted callers.

In addition to tracking phone numbers using phone number lookup services and call logs, Python can also be used to monitor incoming calls in real-time. By integrating Python with a phone system or VoIP service, you can create a custom call tracking system that alerts you

Chapter 11: OSINT Geolocation

Open Source Intelligence (OSINT) geolocation is a powerful tool that allows individuals and organizations to gather information about a specific location using publicly available data sources. By analyzing data such as social media posts, satellite imagery, and online mapping services, OSINT geolocation can provide valuable insights into the physical whereabouts of people, objects, or events.

One of the key benefits of OSINT geolocation is its ability to provide real-time information about a location. By monitoring social media platforms and other online sources, analysts can track the movements of individuals or groups in near real-time. This can be particularly useful for law enforcement agencies, intelligence organizations, and other entities that need to quickly locate and track targets.

OSINT geolocation can also be used to gather information about a location before physically visiting it. By analyzing satellite imagery and other online mapping services, analysts can gain a better understanding of the layout of a specific area, identify potential security risks, and plan their operations more effectively. This can be especially useful for military forces, emergency responders, and humanitarian organizations operating in unfamiliar or hostile environments.

In addition to providing real-time information and pre-visit analysis, OSINT geolocation can also be used to track the movements of individuals or objects over time. By analyzing historical data from social media posts, online transactions, and other sources, analysts can create a detailed timeline of a target's activities and movements. This can be valuable for conducting investigations, monitoring the activities of criminal organizations, or tracking the movements of high-value assets.

One of the key challenges of OSINT geolocation is the need to verify the accuracy of the information gathered. While publicly available data sources can provide valuable insights into a location, they can also be easily manipulated or falsified. Analysts must therefore be diligent in cross-referencing multiple sources, verifying the authenticity of the data, and critically evaluating the reliability of the information before making any operational decisions.

Another challenge of OSINT geolocation is the need to protect the privacy and security of individuals and organizations. By collecting and analyzing publicly available data, analysts may inadvertently expose sensitive information about individuals, such as their home address, daily routines, or personal relationships. It is therefore essential for analysts to adhere to strict ethical guidelines, respect the privacy rights of individuals, and ensure that any information gathered is used responsibly and in accordance with the law.

Despite these challenges, OSINT geolocation remains a valuable tool for gathering information about specific locations. By leveraging publicly available data sources, analysts can gain valuable insights into the physical whereabouts of people, objects, or events, track the movements of targets in real-time, and gather information about a location before physically visiting it. With proper training, ethical guidelines, and critical thinking skills, OSINT geolocation can be a powerful tool for enhancing situational awareness, conducting investigations, and making informed operational decisions.

Using Maps for OSINT

Open Source Intelligence (OSINT) is a valuable tool for gathering information from publicly available sources to support decision-making and analysis. One of the most powerful tools available for OSINT is the use of maps.
Maps can provide a wealth of information, from geographic locations to spatial relationships between different entities. In this article, we will explore how maps can be used effectively for OSINT purposes.

One of the key benefits of using maps for OSINT is the ability to visualize data in a spatial context. By plotting relevant information on a map, analysts can quickly identify patterns, trends, and connections that may not be immediately apparent in a traditional text-based format. For example, mapping the locations of known criminal activities can help law enforcement agencies identify hotspots and allocate resources more effectively.

Maps can also be used to track the movements of individuals or groups over time. By analyzing location data from social media posts, cell phone signals, or other sources, analysts can create a timeline of a person's activities and identify potential patterns or anomalies. This

144

can be particularly useful in tracking the movements of suspects in criminal investigations or monitoring the activities of individuals of interest in national security contexts.

Another valuable use of maps in OSINT is in geospatial analysis. By overlaying multiple layers of data on a map, analysts can identify correlations and relationships between different variables. For example, mapping the locations of known terrorist attacks alongside population density data can help identify potential targets for future attacks. Similarly, mapping the distribution of a particular drug alongside demographic information can help law enforcement agencies target their efforts to combat drug trafficking.

Maps can also be used to monitor and analyze events in real-time. By using tools such as geotagged social media posts or satellite imagery, analysts can track developments on the ground as they unfold. This can be particularly valuable in crisis situations, such as natural disasters or political unrest, where timely information is critical for decision-making.

In addition to their analytical value, maps can also be a powerful communication tool. By visualizing complex data in a clear and intuitive way, maps can help convey information to decision-makers and stakeholders more effectively. For example, presenting a map showing the distribution of a disease outbreak can help public health officials communicate the scope of the problem and plan an appropriate response.

When using maps for OSINT, it is important to consider the reliability and accuracy of the data being used. Not all maps are created equal, and it is important to verify the sources of the data and ensure that it is up-to-date and relevant to the analysis being conducted. Additionally, analysts should be aware of the limitations of maps, such as the potential for bias or inaccuracies in the underlying data.

In conclusion, maps are a valuable tool for OSINT that can provide valuable insights and support decision-making in a wide range of contexts. By visualizing data in a spatial context, tracking movements over time, conducting geospatial analysis, monitoring events in real-time, and communicating information effectively, maps can enhance the effectiveness of OSINT efforts. As technology continues to advance, the use of maps for OSINT is likely to become even more powerful and sophisticated, providing analysts with new ways to gather and analyze information from publicly available sources.

Extracting Geolocation Data – python

Extracting geolocation data is a common task in many applications, such as mapping, location-based services, and geotagging. Geolocation data can provide valuable information about the physical location of a device or user, including latitude, longitude, altitude, and more. In this article, we will discuss how to extract geolocation data using Python, a popular programming language for data analysis and manipulation.

Python has several libraries that can be used to extract

geolocation data from various sources, such as GPS devices, mobile devices, and web services. One of the most commonly used libraries for geolocation data extraction in Python is the `geopy` library. `Geopy` is a Python library that provides geocoding and reverse geocoding capabilities, allowing you to convert addresses into geographic coordinates and vice versa.

To begin extracting geolocation data using Python and the `geopy` library, you first need to install the library. You can do this using the following command:

```
pip install geopy
```

Once you have installed the `geopy` library, you can start using it to extract geolocation data. The first step is to import the necessary modules from the `geopy` library, as shown below:

```python
from geopy.geocoders import Nominatim
```

Next, you need to create an instance of the `Nominatim` geocoder, which is used to perform geocoding operations. The `Nominatim` geocoder is a free and open-source geocoding service provided by OpenStreetMap. You can create an instance of the `Nominatim` geocoder as follows:

```python
```

```
geolocator = Nominatim(user_agent="my_geocoder")
```

In the code snippet above, we created an instance of the
`Nominatim` geocoder with a custom user agent string.
The user agent string is used to identify your application
when making requests to the geocoding service.

Once you have created an instance of the `Nominatim`
geocoder, you can use it to extract geolocation data by
providing an address or location as input. The `geocode`
method of the `Nominatim` geocoder can be used to
geocode a location, as shown in the example below:

```python
location = geolocator.geocode("New York City")
print((location.latitude, location.longitude))
```

In the code snippet above, we used the `geocode` method
of the `Nominatim` geocoder to geocode the location
"New York City." The `geocode` method returns a
`Location` object that contains information about the
geocoded location, including its latitude and longitude
coordinates. We then printed the latitude and longitude
coordinates of the geocoded location.

In addition to geocoding locations, you can also perform
reverse geocoding operations using the `Nominatim`
geocoder. Reverse geocoding allows you to convert
geographic coordinates into human-readable addresses.
You can perform reverse geocoding using the `reverse`
method of the `Nominatim` geocoder, as shown in the

example below:

```python
location = geolocator.reverse("40.7128, -74.0060")
print(location.address)
```

In the code snippet above, we used the `reverse` method of the `Nominatim` geocoder to perform reverse geocoding on the coordinates (40.7128, -74.0060). The `reverse` method returns a `Location` object that contains information about the reverse geocoded address. We then printed the human-readable address of the reverse geocoded location.

In addition to the `Nominatim` geocoder, there are other geocoding services and libraries that you can use to extract geolocation data in Python. One such library is the `geocoder` library, which provides a simple and consistent interface to various geocoding services, such as Google Maps, Bing Maps, and OpenStreetMap.

To use the `geocoder` library to extract geolocation data, you first need to install the library using the following command:

```
pip install geocoder
```

Once you have installed the `geocoder` library, you can start using it to extract geolocation data. The `geocoder` library supports multiple geocoding services, each of which has its own API key requirements and usage limits. To use a specific geocoding service with the `geocoder` library, you need to provide the appropriate API key when creating an instance of the geocoder.

For example, to use the Google Maps geocoding service with the `geocoder` library, you can create an instance of the `GoogleV3` geocoder as follows:

```python
import geocoder g = geocoder.google('New York City', key='
```

Analyzing Satellite Imagery – python

Analyzing satellite imagery using Python has become an essential tool for a wide range of industries, including agriculture, environmental monitoring, urban planning, and disaster response. With the increasing availability of high-resolution satellite data, there is a growing need for efficient and scalable methods to process and analyze this data. Python, with its rich ecosystem of libraries and tools, is well-suited for this task.

One of the most popular libraries for working with satellite imagery in Python is the `rasterio` library. Rasterio is a powerful library for reading and writing geospatial raster data, such as satellite imagery. It provides a simple and intuitive interface for working with raster datasets, making it easy to extract information from satellite images and perform various analysis tasks.

To demonstrate how to analyze satellite imagery using Python, let's consider a simple example of classifying land cover types in a satellite image. We will use a Landsat 8 satellite image of an area in California and classify the land cover into three classes: water, vegetation, and urban areas.

First, we need to download the Landsat 8 image from a public satellite data repository, such as the USGS Earth Explorer. Once we have downloaded the image, we can use the `rasterio` library to open and read the image data. Here is a sample code snippet to read the Landsat 8 image using `rasterio`:

```python
import rasterio

# Open the Landsat 8 image file
with rasterio.open('path/to/landsat_image.tif') as src:
# Read the image data image_data = src.read()
```

Next, we can extract the individual bands of the Landsat 8 image, which contain information about different spectral bands of the electromagnetic spectrum. Landsat 8 images typically consist of 11 bands, each capturing different types of information about the Earth's surface. For our land cover classification task, we will focus on bands 3 (red), 4 (green), and 5 (blue), which are commonly used for vegetation analysis. Here is how we can extract these bands from the Landsat 8 image:

```python
# Extract the red, green, and blue bands from the Landsat
```

```
8 image red_band = image_data[2]
green_band = image_data[3] blue_band = image_data[4]
```

Once we have extracted the red, green, and blue bands from the Landsat 8 image, we can combine them to create a true-color composite image. A true-color composite image is a representation of the satellite image that closely resembles how the human eye perceives the Earth's surface. Here is a code snippet to create a true-color composite image using the red, green, and blue bands:

```python
import numpy as np
import matplotlib.pyplot as plt

# Create a true-color composite image
true_color_image = np.dstack((red_band, green_band, blue_band))

# Display the true-color composite image
plt.imshow(true_color_image) plt.axis('off')
plt.show()
```

The true-color composite image will provide us with a visual representation of the Landsat 8 image, which we can use to identify different land cover types in the image. However, to perform a more quantitative analysis of the land cover types, we need to apply a classification algorithm to the satellite image data.

One of the most commonly used classification algorithms

for analyzing satellite imagery is the supervised classification algorithm. In supervised classification, we train a machine learning model using labeled training data, and then apply the model to classify the remaining pixels in the image. For our land cover classification task, we can use a simple machine learning algorithm, such as the Random Forest classifier, to classify the satellite image into water, vegetation, and urban areas.

Here is a code snippet to train a Random Forest classifier using the red, green, and blue bands of the Landsat 8 image, along with labeled training data for water, vegetation, and urban areas:

```python
from sklearn.ensemble import RandomForestClassifier

# Create labeled training data for water, vegetation, and urban areas training_data = np.concatenate((water_pixels, vegetation_pixels, urban_pixels))
labels = np.concatenate((np.zeros(len(water_pixels)), np.ones(len(vegetation_pixels)), np.full(len(urban_pixels), 2))

# Train a Random Forest classifier classifier = RandomForestClassifier()    classifier.fit(training_data, labels)
```

Once we have trained the Random Forest classifier, we can apply it to classify the remaining pixels in the Landsat 8 image. Here is a code snippet to classify the satellite image using the trained classifier:

```python
# Classify the satellite image using the trained Random
Forest classifier image_shape = red_band.shape
image_data_reshaped                              =
np.column_stack((red_band.flatten(),
green_band.flatten(),            blue_band.flatten()))
predicted_labels                                 =
classifier.predict(image_data_reshaped).reshape
```

Chapter 12: Public Records and Database Searching – OSINT

Public records and database searching, also known as open-source intelligence (OSINT), is the process of gathering information from publicly available sources to obtain valuable insights. This practice has become increasingly popular in recent years due to the vast amount of information that is now accessible online. From social media profiles to court records, there is a wealth of data waiting to be uncovered through public records and database searching.

One of the key benefits of public records and database searching is the ability to access information that may not be readily available through traditional means. For example, if you are conducting a background check on a potential employee, you can use public records to verify their employment history, criminal record, and even their social media activity. This can help you make more informed decisions when hiring new employees or entering into business partnerships.

In addition to background checks, public records and database searching can also be used for a variety of other purposes. For example, law enforcement agencies often use OSINT techniques to gather intelligence on criminal suspects, track down missing persons, and investigate fraudulent activities. Journalists and researchers also rely on public records to uncover hidden connections, track trends, and verify information.

One of the key challenges of public records and database searching is the sheer volume of data that is available. With so much information to sift through, it can be overwhelming to know where to start. Fortunately, there are a variety of tools and techniques that can help streamline the process and ensure that you are able to find the information you need quickly and efficiently.

One of the most common tools used in public records and database searching is a search engine. By entering relevant keywords or phrases, you can quickly uncover a wealth of information on a particular topic or individual. However, search engines can be limited in their capabilities, especially when it comes to accessing more sensitive information such as criminal records or financial data.

To access this type of information, you may need to use specialized databases or search engines that are designed specifically for public records and database searching. These tools can provide access to a wide range of information, including court records, property records, business licenses, and more. By using these tools, you can uncover information that may not be readily available through traditional search engines.

Another important aspect of public records and database searching is ensuring that the information you uncover is accurate and up to date. With so much information available online, it can be easy to become overwhelmed by conflicting or outdated information. To avoid this, it is important to verify the sources of your information and cross-reference it with multiple sources whenever possible.

In addition to verifying the accuracy of your information, it is also important to consider the ethical implications of public records and database searching. While it can be tempting to use OSINT techniques to uncover personal information about individuals, it is important to respect their privacy and only use this information for legitimate purposes. By following ethical guidelines and using public records and database searching responsibly, you can ensure that you are able to gather valuable insights without infringing on the rights of others.

Overall, public records and database searching is a powerful tool that can provide valuable insights for a wide range of purposes. From background checks to investigative journalism, there are countless ways that OSINT techniques can be used to uncover information and make more informed decisions. By using the right tools and techniques, you can harness the power of public records and database searching to access the information you need quickly and efficiently.

Accessing Public Records - OSINT

Accessing public records is a crucial aspect of open-source intelligence (OSINT) gathering, and Python is a powerful tool that can be used to automate and streamline the process. By leveraging Python's libraries and modules, researchers and investigators can efficiently retrieve and analyze a wide range of public records, including court documents, property records, business filings, and more.

Python is a popular programming language that is widely used in data analysis, web scraping, and automation tasks. Its simplicity and versatility make it an ideal choice for accessing public records, as it allows users to quickly develop custom scripts and tools to extract information from various sources.

One of the key benefits of using Python for accessing public records is its ability to handle large volumes of data quickly and efficiently. By writing scripts that automate the retrieval and processing of public records, researchers can save time and effort compared to manual methods.

There are several libraries and modules in Python that can be used to access public records. One of the most commonly used libraries is BeautifulSoup, which is a web scraping library that allows users to extract data from HTML and XML files. BeautifulSoup makes it easy to parse and navigate through web pages, making it an essential tool for accessing public records stored on websites.

Another popular library for accessing public records in Python is Requests, which is used to send HTTP requests and retrieve data from websites. Requests is a versatile library that supports various types of requests, including GET and POST requests, making it ideal for interacting with web-based public record databases.

In addition to BeautifulSoup and Requests, there are several other libraries in Python that can be used for accessing public records. For example, Pandas can be used to manipulate and analyze data retrieved from public record sources, while NumPy can be used for numerical analysis and data processing.

When accessing public records using Python, it is important to be aware of any legal and ethical considerations. While many public records are freely available for anyone to access, some records may be restricted or require permission to access. Researchers should always ensure that they have the right to access and use the information they retrieve, and should respect any privacy or confidentiality restrictions that may apply.

In addition to legal considerations, researchers should also be mindful of the accuracy and reliability of the public records they access. While public records are generally considered to be trustworthy sources of information, errors and inaccuracies can occur, so it is important to verify the information obtained from public record sources before relying on it for decision-making or investigative purposes.

To access public records using Python, researchers can follow a few simple steps. First, they should identify the specific public records they are interested in accessing, such as court documents, property records, or business filings. Once the target records have been identified, researchers can search for online databases or websites that provide access to the desired records.

Next, researchers can use Python to write a script that automates the process of retrieving and analyzing the public records. This script can use libraries such as BeautifulSoup and Requests to access and extract data from the target websites, and can use Pandas and NumPy to process and analyze the retrieved data.

For example, if a researcher is interested in accessing property records for a specific location, they can write a Python script that sends a series of requests to a property records database, retrieves the relevant data, and stores it in a Pandas DataFrame for further analysis. The researcher can then use NumPy to perform statistical analysis on the property records data, such as calculating average property values or identifying trends in property ownership.

Overall, accessing public records using Python is a powerful and efficient way to gather information for research, investigation, and decision-making purposes. By leveraging Python's libraries and modules, researchers can automate the process of retrieving and analyzing public records, saving time and effort compared to manual methods. However, researchers should always be mindful of legal and ethical considerations when accessing public records, and should verify the accuracy and reliability of the information obtained from public record sources.

Searching Government Databases – Python

Python is a powerful programming language that is widely used for various applications, including data analysis, web development, and automation. One area where Python is particularly useful is in searching government databases. Government databases contain a wealth of information that can be valuable for research, analysis, and decision-making. By using Python to search government databases, users can automate the process of retrieving and analyzing data, making it faster and more efficient.

There are many government databases that can be accessed and searched using Python. Some examples include the United States Census Bureau's database, the Federal Election Commission's database of campaign finance data, and the Centers for Disease Control and Prevention's database of health statistics. These databases contain a wide range of information on topics such as demographics, economics, politics, and health, making them valuable resources for researchers, policymakers, and the general public.

One of the key advantages of using Python to search government databases is that it allows users to automate the process of retrieving and analyzing data. Instead of manually searching through a database and extracting information, users can write Python scripts that automatically query the database, retrieve the relevant data, and perform analysis on it. This can save a significant amount of time and effort, especially when dealing with large or complex datasets.

Python has a number of libraries and tools that make it easy to search government databases. One popular library for working with databases in Python is SQLAlchemy, which provides a high-level interface for interacting with relational databases. SQLAlchemy allows users to write SQL queries in Python code, making it easy to retrieve and manipulate data from a database. Another useful library is Pandas, which provides data structures and functions for working with structured data, such as tables and spreadsheets.

In addition to libraries like SQLAlchemy and Pandas, Python also has tools for working with specific types of databases. For example, the psycopg2 library can be used to connect to and query PostgreSQL databases, while the sqlite3 library can be used to work with SQLite databases. These tools make it easy to search and retrieve data from a wide range of government databases, regardless of the specific technology they use.

To search a government database using Python, users typically follow a few key steps. First, they establish a connection to the database using a library like SQLAlchemy or psycopg2. Next, they write a SQL query to retrieve the desired data from the database. This query can be as simple or complex as needed, depending on the specific information being sought. Once the data has been retrieved, users can then analyze it using Python code, visualize it using tools like Matplotlib or Seaborn, or save it to a file for further analysis.

Searching government databases using Python can be particularly useful for researchers and policymakers who need to access and analyze large amounts of data. For example, a researcher studying trends in income inequality might use Python to search the Census Bureau's database for data on household income over time. By automating the process of retrieving and analyzing this data, the researcher can quickly identify patterns and trends that would be difficult to uncover manually.

In addition to researchers and policymakers, Python can also be useful for journalists and activists who need to access and analyze government data for investigative reporting or advocacy purposes. For example, a journalist investigating corruption in campaign finance might use Python to search the Federal Election Commission's database for suspicious patterns in campaign contributions. By automating the process of searching and analyzing this data, the journalist can uncover important information that can be used to hold politicians and donors accountable.

Overall, Python is a powerful tool for searching government databases. By automating the process of retrieving and analyzing data, users can save time and effort, and uncover valuable insights that would be difficult to find manually. Whether you are a researcher, policymaker, journalist, or activist, Python can help you access and analyze government data in a fast and efficient way. With its wide range of libraries and tools for working with databases, Python is a valuable resource for anyone who needs to search government databases for information.

Extracting Data from Open Repositories

In today's digital age, data is king. Businesses and organizations rely on data to make informed decisions, drive innovation, and stay ahead of the competition. With the vast amount of data available on the internet, extracting and analyzing data has become a crucial task for many industries. Open repositories, such as GitHub, provide a treasure trove of data that can be leveraged for various purposes. In this article, we will explore how to extract data from open repositories using Python examples.

Python is a popular programming language known for its simplicity and versatility. It has a rich ecosystem of libraries and tools that make it ideal for data extraction and analysis. With Python, you can easily access and extract data from open repositories like GitHub, Bitbucket, and more.

To extract data from open repositories using Python, you first need to understand the basics of web scraping. Web scraping is the process of extracting data from websites and storing it in a structured format. There are several libraries in Python that can help you with web scraping, such as BeautifulSoup, Scrapy, and Requests.

Let's take a look at an example of how to extract data from GitHub using Python. GitHub is a popular platform for hosting and sharing code repositories. You can use the GitHub API to access data from repositories, users, organizations, and more.

First, you need to install the requests library, which will allow you to make HTTP requests to the GitHub API. You can install the requests library using pip:

```
```

pip install requests
```
```

Next, you need to generate a personal access token from your GitHub account. This token will be used to authenticate your requests to the GitHub API. You can generate a personal access token by following the instructions on the GitHub website.

Once you have your personal access token, you can use it to authenticate your requests to the GitHub API. Here is an example of how to extract data from a GitHub repository using Python:

```python
import requests

# Replace 'YOUR_ACCESS_TOKEN' with your personal access token headers = {'Authorization': 'token YOUR_ACCESS_TOKEN'}

# URL of the GitHub repository
url = 'https://api.github.com/repos/username/repository'

# Make a GET request to the GitHub API response = requests.get(url, headers=headers)

# Check if the request was successful
if response.status_code == 200:
```

```
# Extract the data from the response data =
response.json()
# Print the data print(data)
else:
print('Error: Unable to retrieve data from GitHub')
```

In this example, we are making a GET request to the GitHub API to retrieve data from a specific repository. We are passing our personal access token in the headers of the request to authenticate ourselves. If the request is successful, we extract the data from the response and print it to the console.

You can also extract data from other endpoints of the GitHub API, such as users, organizations, and more. The GitHub API documentation provides a comprehensive list of endpoints and parameters that you can use to extract data from GitHub.

In addition to extracting data from GitHub, you can also extract data from other open repositories using Python. For example, you can use the BeautifulSoup library to scrape data from websites and store it in a structured format. Here is an example of how to extract data from a website using BeautifulSoup:

```python
from bs4 import BeautifulSoup import requests

# URL of the website
url = 'https://example.com'
```

```python
# Make a GET request to the website response =
requests.get(url)

# Check if the request was successful if
response.status_code == 200:
# Parse the HTML content of the website
soup = BeautifulSoup(response.content, 'html.parser') #
Extract the data from the website
data = soup.find('div', class_='content').text # Print the
data
print(data) else:
print('Error: Unable to retrieve data from the website')
```

In this example, we are using the BeautifulSoup library to parse the HTML content of a website and extract data from it. We are making a GET request to the website and parsing the HTML content using BeautifulSoup. We then extract the data from a specific element of the website and print it to the console.

In conclusion, extracting data from open repositories using Python is a powerful tool that can help you access and analyze data for various purposes. With Python, you can easily extract data from GitHub, websites, and other repositories, and store it in a structured format for further analysis. By leveraging the rich ecosystem of libraries and tools available in Python, you can streamline the data extraction process and gain valuable insights from open repositories. So, roll up your sleeves, fire up your Python interpreter, and start extracting data from open repositories today!

Chapter 13: Network OSINT Analysis

Network OSINT (Open Source Intelligence) analysis is a crucial aspect of cybersecurity and threat intelligence. It involves gathering and analyzing information from publicly available sources to gain insights into potential threats, vulnerabilities, and risks that may affect an organization's network. By leveraging OSINT techniques, security professionals can proactively identify and mitigate security threats before they escalate into major incidents.

One of the key benefits of Network OSINT analysis is its ability to provide a comprehensive view of an organization's network environment. By collecting information from various sources such as social media, forums, blogs, and websites, security analysts can gain a better understanding of the potential risks and vulnerabilities that may exist within the network. This information can help organizations make informed decisions about their security posture and develop effective strategies to protect their assets.

Network OSINT analysis can also help organizations identify potential threats and malicious actors that may be targeting their network. By monitoring online activities and discussions, security analysts can identify indicators of compromise (IOCs) and suspicious behavior that may indicate a security breach. This information can be used to proactively detect and respond to threats before they cause significant damage to the network.

In addition to threat intelligence, Network OSINT analysis can also provide valuable insights into the security practices of other organizations in the industry. By monitoring the online activities of competitors and industry peers, organizations can gain valuable information about emerging threats, vulnerabilities, and best practices for securing their network. This information can help organizations benchmark their security posture against industry standards and identify areas for improvement.

To conduct effective Network OSINT analysis, security professionals must have a solid understanding of the tools and techniques used to gather and analyze information from publicly available sources. There are a variety of tools and platforms available that can help automate the process of collecting and analyzing OSINT data, such as social media monitoring tools, web scraping tools, and threat intelligence platforms.

One of the key challenges of Network OSINT analysis is the sheer volume of data that must be collected and analyzed. With the proliferation of online sources and platforms, security analysts must be able to filter through vast amounts of information to identify relevant and actionable intelligence. This requires a combination of technical skills, analytical thinking, and domain expertise to effectively interpret and prioritize OSINT data.

Another challenge of Network OSINT analysis is the need to ensure the accuracy and reliability of the information collected. Since OSINT data is sourced from publicly available sources, there is a risk of misinformation, false positives, and outdated information. Security analysts must be able to verify the credibility of the sources and cross-reference information to ensure its accuracy before making any decisions based on the intelligence gathered.

In conclusion, Network OSINT analysis is a critical component of cybersecurity and threat intelligence that can provide organizations with valuable insights into potential threats, vulnerabilities, and risks that may affect their network. By leveraging OSINT techniques, security professionals can proactively identify and mitigate security threats, improve their security posture, and stay ahead of emerging threats in the ever-evolving cybersecurity landscape. Effective Network OSINT analysis requires a combination of technical skills, analytical thinking, and domain expertise to gather, analyze, and interpret OSINT data accurately and effectively.

Gathering Data from Shodan – Python

Shodan is a popular search engine for finding and gathering information on internet-connected devices. It allows users to search for specific types of devices, such as webcams, routers, servers, and more, by using various filters and search queries. In this article, we will explore how to gather data from Shodan using Python, a powerful programming language that is commonly used for web scraping and data analysis.

To get started with gathering data from Shodan, you will first need to create a Shodan account and obtain an API key. This key is required to access the Shodan API, which allows you to search for devices and retrieve information about them. You can sign up for a free Shodan account on their website and obtain an API key from your account settings.

Once you have your API key, you can start using the Shodan API in Python by installing the Shodan library. You can do this by running the following command in your terminal or command prompt:

```
```

pip install shodan
```
```

This will install the Shodan library, which provides a convenient interface for interacting with the Shodan API in Python. You can now start writing Python code to search for devices and gather data from Shodan.

To search for devices using the Shodan API, you can use the `shodan.Shodan` class provided by the Shodan library. Here is an example code snippet that shows how to search for devices with a specific query:

```python
import shodan

# Initialize the Shodan API client api_key = "YOUR_API_KEY" api = shodan.Shodan(api_key)

# Define the search query query = "webcam"

# Perform the search results = api.search(query)
```

```
# Print the results
for result in results['matches']:
print(result)
```

In this code snippet, we first import the `shodan` library and initialize the Shodan API client with our API key. We then define a search query for devices with the keyword "webcam" and perform the search using the `api.search()` method. The results are stored in the `results` variable, which is a dictionary containing information about the devices that match the search query. We then iterate over the results and print out each device's

information.

You can customize the search query by using various filters and search operators supported by the Shodan API. For example, you can search for devices with specific ports open, operating systems, countries, and more. The Shodan documentation provides a list of supported filters and search operators that you can use to refine your search queries.

In addition to searching for devices, you can also retrieve detailed information about a specific device by its IP address using the `api.host()` method. Here is an example code snippet that shows how to retrieve information about a specific device:

```python
```

```
# Define the target IP address target_ip = "8.8.8.8"

# Retrieve information about the target device host =
api.host(target_ip)

# Print the information print(host)
```

In this code snippet, we specify the target IP address of the device we want to retrieve information about and use the `api.host()` method to fetch the device's details. The information is stored in the `host` variable, which is a dictionary containing various attributes of the device, such as its IP address, ports, operating system, and more. We then print out the information to the console.

Once you have gathered data from Shodan, you can analyze and visualize it using various data analysis and visualization libraries in Python, such as `pandas`, `matplotlib`, and `seaborn`. You can also store the data in a database or a CSV file for further analysis and reporting.

In conclusion, gathering data from Shodan using Python is a powerful way to discover and analyze information about internet-connected devices. By leveraging the Shodan API and Python programming language, you can search for devices, retrieve detailed information about them, and perform data analysis to gain insights into the security and configuration of these devices. With the right tools and techniques, you can uncover valuable information and make informed decisions to secure your network and infrastructure.

173

Analyzing Network Traffic - OSINT – Python

Analyzing network traffic is a critical aspect of cybersecurity, as it allows organizations to monitor and detect potential threats on their networks. Open-source intelligence (OSINT) is a valuable tool for gathering information about network traffic, and Python is a popular programming language for analyzing and processing this data. In this article, we will explore how Python can be used to analyze network traffic using OSINT techniques.

Network traffic analysis involves monitoring and analyzing the data that flows through a network. This data can include information about the devices connected to the network, the type of traffic being transmitted, and any potential security threats. By analyzing network traffic, organizations can identify abnormal behavior, detect potential security breaches, and take proactive measures to protect their networks.

Open-source intelligence (OSINT) refers to the practice of gathering information from publicly available sources, such as social media, websites, and online forums. OSINT can be a valuable tool for analyzing network traffic, as it can provide additional context and insights into the data being analyzed. By combining network traffic analysis with OSINT techniques, organizations can gain a more comprehensive understanding of their network activity and potential security threats.

Python is a versatile programming language that is widely used in the field of cybersecurity. Its simplicity and readability make it an ideal choice for analyzing network traffic and processing large amounts of data. Python also has a wide range of libraries and tools that can be used to analyze network traffic, such as Scapy, Pyshark, and NetworkX.

One of the key benefits of using Python for network traffic analysis is its ability to automate the process. By writing scripts and programs in Python, cybersecurity professionals can quickly and efficiently analyze large volumes of network traffic data. This can help organizations to detect and respond to security threats in real- time, minimizing the impact of potential breaches.

To analyze network traffic using Python and OSINT techniques, cybersecurity professionals can follow a few key steps:

Collecting network traffic data: The first step in analyzing network traffic is to collect data from the network. This can be done using tools such as Wireshark, tcpdump, or Bro IDS. These tools capture packets of data as they flow through the network, providing valuable insights into the type of traffic being transmitted.

Preprocessing the data: Once the network traffic data has been collected, it needs to be preprocessed before it can be analyzed. This may involve filtering out irrelevant data, converting data formats, and cleaning up any inconsistencies in the data.

Analyzing the data: With the data preprocessed, cybersecurity professionals can begin analyzing the network traffic using Python. This may involve identifying patterns in the data, detecting anomalies, and correlating data from different sources to gain a comprehensive understanding of the network activity.

Visualizing the data: Visualization is an important aspect of network traffic analysis, as it can help cybersecurity professionals to identify trends and patterns in the data. Python has a range of libraries, such as Matplotlib and Seaborn, that can be used to create visualizations of network traffic data.

Applying OSINT techniques: To enhance the analysis of network traffic data, cybersecurity professionals can leverage OSINT techniques to gather additional information about the data being analyzed. This may involve querying public databases, searching for information on social media platforms, or monitoring online forums for relevant discussions.

By combining Python with OSINT techniques, cybersecurity professionals can gain a deeper understanding of their network traffic and identify potential security threats. This can help organizations to proactively protect their networks and respond quickly to any security incidents.

In conclusion, analyzing network traffic using Python and OSINT techniques is a valuable practice for cybersecurity professionals. By automating the analysis process, leveraging OSINT techniques, and visualizing the data, organizations can gain valuable insights into their network activity and detect potential security threats. Python's versatility and simplicity make it an ideal choice for network traffic analysis, and cybersecurity professionals can use it to enhance their cybersecurity defenses and protect their networks from potential threats.

Cybersecurity OSINT Tools - Advanced lists

Cybersecurity OSINT (Open Source Intelligence) tools are essential for organizations and individuals to gather information about potential threats and vulnerabilities in their systems. These tools provide valuable insights into the activities of cybercriminals and help in identifying and mitigating risks before they can cause harm.

In this article, we will discuss some of the advanced Cybersecurity OSINT tools that are widely used by security professionals to enhance their threat intelligence capabilities.

Maltego:

Maltego is a powerful OSINT tool that allows users to visualize and analyze complex relationships in data. It can be used to gather information from various sources, including social media platforms, websites, and public databases. Maltego's intuitive interface makes it easy to map out connections between different entities, such as people, organizations, and domains.

Shodan:

Shodan is a search engine that allows users to find internet-connected devices, including servers, routers, and cameras. This tool can be used to identify vulnerable systems that are exposed to the internet and may be targeted by attackers. Shodan provides detailed information about each device, including its location, operating system, and open ports.

SpiderFoot:

SpiderFoot is an open-source OSINT tool that automates the process of gathering information about a target. It can be used to collect data from a wide range of sources, including social media platforms, domain registration records, and public databases. SpiderFoot's modular design allows users to customize the tool to suit their specific needs.

Recon-ng:

Recon-ng is a powerful OSINT tool that is specifically designed for reconnaissance and information gathering. It can be used to collect data from a variety of sources, such as search engines, social media platforms, and public databases. Recon-ng's flexible framework allows users to create custom modules to extract information from specific websites or services.

theHarvester:

theHarvester is a popular OSINT tool that is used to gather email addresses, subdomains, and other information about a target. It can be used to conduct reconnaissance on a target organization or individual and identify potential attack vectors. theHarvester supports multiple data sources, including search engines, social media platforms, and public databases.

Censys:

Censys is a search engine that allows users to find internet-connected devices and networks. It can be used to identify vulnerable systems that are exposed to the internet and may be targeted by attackers. Censys provides detailed information about each device, including its location, operating system, and open ports.

OSINT Framework:

OSINT Framework is a comprehensive collection of OSINT tools and resources that are organized into different categories, such as social media, search engines, and public databases. It provides a centralized repository of tools that can be used to gather information about a target from various sources. OSINT Framework's user- friendly interface makes it easy to navigate and find the right tool for a specific task.

Datasploit:

Datasploit is an OSINT tool that is designed to automate the process of gathering information about a target. It can be used to collect data from a variety of sources, including social media platforms, domain registration records, and public databases. Datasploit's modular design allows users to customize the tool to suit their specific needs.

Sniper:

Sniper is a reconnaissance and vulnerability assessment tool that is designed for penetration testers and security professionals. It can be used to gather information about a target, such as open ports, services, and vulnerabilities. Sniper's automated scanning capabilities make it easy to identify potential attack vectors and prioritize remediation efforts.

Metagoofil:

Metagoofil is an OSINT tool that is used to extract metadata from files that are publicly available on the internet. It can be used to gather information about a target organization or individual, such as email addresses, usernames, and document titles. Metagoofil's simple interface makes it easy to search for files and extract metadata from them.

In conclusion, Cybersecurity OSINT tools are essential for organizations and individuals to gather information about potential threats and vulnerabilities in their systems. The advanced tools mentioned in this article provide valuable insights into the activities of cybercriminals and help in identifying and mitigating risks before they can cause harm. By leveraging these tools effectively, security professionals can enhance their threat intelligence capabilities and stay one step ahead of cyber threats.

Chapter 14: Integrating OSINT into Pentesting

Integrating open-source intelligence (OSINT) into penetration testing, or pentesting, is essential for conducting thorough and effective security assessments. OSINT refers to the collection and analysis of publicly available information to gather intelligence about a target organization or individual. By incorporating OSINT tools and techniques into the pentesting process, security professionals can enhance their understanding of potential vulnerabilities and threats, leading to more comprehensive and successful assessments.

One of the key benefits of integrating OSINT into pentesting is the ability to gather valuable information about the target organization's digital footprint. This includes details such as domain names, IP addresses, email addresses, social media profiles, and other online assets that can be leveraged by attackers to exploit vulnerabilities. By conducting OSINT research, pentesters can identify potential entry points into the target network and develop targeted attack strategies to simulate real-world threats.

OSINT can also provide valuable insights into the target organization's employees, partners, and vendors. By analyzing publicly available information about key personnel, such as job titles, responsibilities, and contact details, pentesters can identify potential points of contact for social engineering attacks. Additionally, OSINT research can reveal information about third-party relationships, such as suppliers and service providers, that may introduce additional security risks to the target organization.

Furthermore, OSINT can help pentesters identify potential security misconfigurations and vulnerabilities in the target organization's external infrastructure. By analyzing publicly available information about the target organization's domain names, IP addresses, and network architecture, pentesters can identify potential weak points that could be exploited by attackers. This information can be used to prioritize and focus testing efforts on the most critical areas of the target network, leading to more efficient and effective security assessments.

In addition to gathering intelligence about the target organization, OSINT can also be used to identify potential threats and vulnerabilities in the broader security landscape. By monitoring online forums, social media platforms, and other sources of public information, pentesters can stay informed about emerging security trends, techniques, and tools used by attackers. This knowledge can be used to enhance testing methodologies, develop new attack vectors, and improve overall security posture.

To effectively integrate OSINT into pentesting, security professionals should leverage a variety of tools and techniques to gather, analyze, and interpret publicly available information. This may include using specialized OSINT tools and search engines to collect data, conducting manual research to verify and validate findings, and employing data analysis techniques to identify patterns and trends. By combining these methods, pentesters can develop a comprehensive understanding of the target organization and its potential security risks.

It is important to note that while OSINT can provide valuable insights into potential vulnerabilities and threats, it should be used in conjunction with other pentesting methodologies, such as network scanning, vulnerability assessment, and social engineering. By combining OSINT with these techniques, security professionals can conduct more thorough and realistic security assessments that accurately reflect the capabilities and motivations of real-world attackers.

Integrating OSINT into pentesting is essential for conducting comprehensive and effective security assessments. By leveraging publicly available information to gather intelligence about the target organization, employees, partners, and vendors, security professionals can identify potential vulnerabilities, threats, and security risks that may be exploited by attackers. By combining OSINT with other pentesting methodologies, such as network scanning and social engineering, security professionals can develop a holistic testing approach that simulates real-world threats and helps organizations improve their overall security posture.

Ethical Considerations X Blackhat

When it comes to the world of cybersecurity, ethical considerations are of utmost importance. One of the most controversial topics within this realm is that of blackhat hacking. Blackhat hacking is the practice of using hacking techniques for malicious purposes, such as stealing personal information, disrupting systems, or causing harm to individuals or organizations.

Ethical considerations in blackhat hacking are complex and multifaceted. On one hand, some argue that blackhat hackers are simply exploiting vulnerabilities in systems in order to expose weaknesses and improve security.
They believe that these hackers play a crucial role in identifying and fixing security flaws that might otherwise go unnoticed.

However, the majority of cybersecurity experts and professionals strongly condemn blackhat hacking due to its inherently malicious nature. Blackhat hackers often engage in criminal activities, such as identity theft, financial fraud, and cyber espionage. These actions can have devastating consequences for individuals, businesses, and even entire countries.

From an ethical standpoint, blackhat hacking raises a number of important considerations. Firstly, there is the issue of consent. When a blackhat hacker breaches a system or steals sensitive information, they are violating the privacy and security of the individuals or organizations involved. This lack of consent is a clear violation of ethical principles and can have serious legal consequences.

Additionally, blackhat hacking can cause significant harm to innocent individuals who may become victims of cyber attacks. For example, a hacker who steals personal information from a company's database could use that information to commit identity theft or financial fraud. This can have far-reaching consequences for the individuals affected, including financial loss, damage to their reputation, and emotional distress.

Furthermore, blackhat hacking can also have negative implications for the cybersecurity industry as a whole. By engaging in unethical and illegal activities, blackhat hackers undermine the trust and credibility of legitimate cybersecurity professionals. This can make it more difficult for organizations to protect themselves against cyber threats and can ultimately harm the overall security of the digital landscape.

In order to address these ethical considerations, it is essential for individuals and organizations to take a strong stance against blackhat hacking. This includes implementing robust cybersecurity measures to protect against potential attacks, as well as educating employees and users about the importance of ethical behavior online.

It is also important for law enforcement agencies and cybersecurity professionals to work together to identify and prosecute blackhat hackers who engage in criminal activities. By holding these individuals accountable for their actions, we can send a clear message that unethical behavior in the digital realm will not be tolerated.

In conclusion, ethical considerations in blackhat hacking are of critical importance in the field of cybersecurity. By understanding the ethical implications of these actions and taking proactive steps to prevent them, we can help to protect individuals, organizations, and society as a whole from the harmful effects of cyber attacks. It is essential for all stakeholders to work together to uphold ethical standards and promote a safe and secure digital environment for all.

Reporting and Documentation – OSINT

Reporting and documentation are essential components of Open Source Intelligence (OSINT) operations. OSINT involves collecting and analyzing information from publicly available sources to gather intelligence on a particular subject or target. Proper reporting and documentation of OSINT findings are crucial for ensuring the accuracy, reliability, and credibility of the intelligence gathered.

When conducting OSINT operations, it is important to keep detailed records of the sources of information, the methods used to collect the data, and the analysis performed on the data. This documentation is necessary to verify the accuracy of the information and to provide a clear trail of evidence for future reference. Reporting on OSINT findings involves summarizing the key findings, analyzing the information gathered, and presenting the intelligence in a clear and concise manner.

One of the key benefits of proper reporting and documentation in OSINT is the ability to share intelligence with other analysts, researchers, or decision-makers. By documenting the sources and methods used to collect and analyze the data, other individuals can verify the accuracy of the information and build upon the intelligence gathered. This collaboration and sharing of information are essential for creating a more comprehensive and accurate picture of a particular subject or target.

In addition to sharing intelligence with others, proper reporting and documentation in OSINT can also help in identifying gaps in the information collected and areas for further research. By keeping detailed records of the sources of information and the analysis performed, analysts can identify areas where additional data is needed or where further investigation is required. This can help in refining the research process and ensuring that all relevant information is considered in the analysis.

Furthermore, proper reporting and documentation in OSINT can also help in assessing the reliability and credibility of the information gathered. By documenting the sources of information and the methods used to collect the data, analysts can evaluate the trustworthiness of the sources and the accuracy of the information. This is crucial for ensuring that the intelligence gathered is reliable and can be used confidently in decision-making processes.

There are several best practices to follow when reporting and documenting OSINT findings. Firstly, it is important to keep detailed records of the sources of information, including the URLs of websites, the names of individuals or organizations providing the information, and any other relevant details. This can help in verifying the accuracy of the information and in providing a clear trail of evidence for future reference.

Secondly, it is important to document the methods used to collect and analyze the data. This includes detailing the search terms used, the tools and techniques employed, and

187

any other relevant information about the research process. By documenting the methods used, analysts can ensure that the data is collected and analyzed in a systematic and rigorous manner.

Lastly, it is important to summarize the key findings and analysis in a clear and concise report. This report should include a summary of the information gathered, an analysis of the data, and any conclusions or recommendations based on the intelligence. By presenting the information in a structured and organized manner, analysts can communicate their findings effectively to others and facilitate decision-making processes.

In conclusion, reporting and documentation are essential components of OSINT operations. By keeping detailed records of the sources of information, the methods used to collect and analyze the data, and summarizing the key findings in a clear and concise report, analysts can ensure the accuracy, reliability, and credibility of the intelligence gathered.

Proper reporting and documentation also facilitate collaboration and sharing of information with others, help in identifying gaps in the information collected, and assess the reliability and credibility of the data. By following best practices in reporting and documentation, analysts can enhance the effectiveness and impact of their OSINT operations.

OSINT Automation

Open Source Intelligence (OSINT) is a valuable tool for gathering information from publicly available sources such as social media, news websites, and government databases. It can provide valuable insights for businesses, government agencies, and individuals looking to gather intelligence on a wide range of topics.

One of the challenges of OSINT is the sheer volume of data that needs to be sifted through to find relevant information. This is where automation comes in. By using automation tools and techniques, analysts can streamline the process of collecting and analyzing data, allowing them to focus on interpreting the results rather than spending hours manually collecting information.

There are several ways in which automation can be used to enhance the OSINT process. One common technique is web scraping, which involves automatically extracting data from websites and other online sources. This can be done using specialized tools or by writing custom scripts that can gather specific types of information from targeted websites.

Another useful automation technique is data enrichment, which involves enhancing the information gathered from OSINT sources with additional data from other sources. For example, analysts can use automation tools to cross-reference social media profiles with public records databases to gather more information about a particular individual.

Automation can also be used to monitor online sources for specific keywords or topics of interest. By setting up automated alerts, analysts can receive notifications whenever new information related to their research is published online. This can help ensure that analysts stay up to date on the latest developments in their field of interest.

In addition to these techniques, automation can also be used to streamline the process of analyzing and visualizing data. By using tools such as machine learning algorithms and data visualization software, analysts can quickly identify patterns and trends in large datasets, allowing them to draw meaningful insights from the information they have gathered.

Overall, automation can significantly enhance the effectiveness and efficiency of the OSINT process. By automating routine tasks such as data collection, enrichment, and analysis, analysts can focus their time and energy on interpreting the results and making informed decisions based on the intelligence they have gathered.

In conclusion, OSINT automation is a powerful tool for enhancing the effectiveness of intelligence gathering and analysis. By using automation techniques to streamline the process of collecting, analyzing, and visualizing data, analysts can save time and resources while improving the quality of their intelligence reports.

Chapter 15: OSINT Automation Scripts – Python

Open Source Intelligence (OSINT) is a valuable tool for gathering information from publicly available sources on the internet. OSINT can be used for a variety of purposes, including intelligence gathering, threat intelligence, and competitive analysis. However, manually collecting and analyzing OSINT data can be time-consuming and labor-intensive. This is where automation scripts come in.

Python is a popular programming language that is widely used for automation tasks due to its simplicity and versatility. With Python, developers can easily create scripts to automate the collection and analysis of OSINT data. In this article, we will discuss how to create OSINT automation scripts using Python.

One of the key benefits of using automation scripts for OSINT is the ability to gather large amounts of data quickly and efficiently. By automating the process of collecting data from various sources, analysts can save time and focus on analyzing the information rather than spending hours manually collecting it.

There are several ways in which Python can be used to automate OSINT tasks. One common approach is to use web scraping libraries such as BeautifulSoup or Scrapy to extract data from websites. These libraries allow developers to programmatically navigate websites, extract specific data points, and store the information in a structured format.

Another approach is to use APIs to access data from social media platforms, search engines, and other online sources. Many websites and platforms offer APIs that allow developers to access their data programmatically. By using APIs, developers can automate the process of collecting data from multiple sources and consolidate it into a single database for analysis.

In addition to web scraping and API access, Python can also be used to automate the analysis of OSINT data. For example, developers can create scripts to search for specific keywords or patterns within a dataset, extract relevant information, and generate reports or alerts based on the findings.

One of the challenges of OSINT automation is the need to continuously update scripts to adapt to changes in websites, APIs, and data formats. Websites frequently update their layouts, APIs change their endpoints, and data formats evolve over time. Developers must be prepared to monitor these changes and update their scripts accordingly to ensure that they continue to function properly.

To address this challenge, developers can use libraries such as Requests-HTML or Selenium to automate the process of interacting with websites and handling dynamic content. These libraries provide tools for navigating websites, interacting with forms, and handling JavaScript-driven content, making it easier to adapt scripts to changes in web environments.

In addition to monitoring changes in websites and APIs, developers must also consider the ethical and legal implications of OSINT automation. It is important to respect the terms of service of websites and APIs, as well as relevant privacy laws and regulations. Developers should ensure that their scripts do not violate any terms of service agreements or infringe on the privacy rights of individuals.

In conclusion, OSINT automation scripts can be a valuable tool for gathering and analyzing information from publicly available sources on the internet. Python is a powerful programming language that can be used to create automation scripts for OSINT tasks, including web scraping, API access, and data analysis. By leveraging Python and related libraries, developers can save time, improve efficiency, and enhance the quality of their OSINT analysis. However, it is important to stay informed about changes in websites, APIs, and data formats, as well as to adhere to ethical and legal guidelines when using automation scripts for OSINT purposes.

Scheduling and Running Automated Tasks

Scheduling and running automated tasks in OSINT (Open Source Intelligence) using Python can greatly enhance the efficiency and effectiveness of gathering intelligence from various sources on the internet. OSINT is a valuable tool for gathering information from publicly available sources, such as social media, websites, and online forums, to support decision-making and investigation processes. By automating the process of collecting and analyzing data, analysts can save time and resources while ensuring a more consistent and thorough approach to intelligence gathering.

Python is a popular programming language that is widely used for automation tasks due to its simplicity and versatility. With Python, analysts can easily create scripts that can scrape websites, interact with APIs, and process data to extract relevant information for intelligence purposes. By utilizing Python libraries such as Requests, BeautifulSoup, and Pandas, analysts can automate the process of collecting and analyzing data from various online sources.

One of the key benefits of using Python for OSINT automation is the ability to schedule and run tasks at specific times or intervals. This allows analysts to set up automated processes that can run in the background without manual intervention, ensuring that intelligence gathering efforts are consistently maintained and updated. By using Python's built-in scheduling libraries such as Schedule or APScheduler, analysts can easily create scripts that can be run at specified times or intervals, such as daily, weekly, or monthly.

To schedule and run automated tasks in OSINT using Python, analysts can follow these steps:

Define the task: The first step in automating an OSINT task is to define the specific task that needs to be automated. This could be anything from scraping a website for specific information to monitoring social media platforms for relevant updates.

Write the script: Once the task has been defined, analysts can write a Python script that will perform the necessary actions to collect and analyze the data. This script can utilize Python libraries such as Requests to interact with websites, BeautifulSoup to parse HTML content, and Pandas to process and analyze the data.

Schedule the task: After the script has been written, analysts can use Python's scheduling libraries to set up a schedule for running the script at specific times or intervals. This can be done by specifying the task to be run at a certain time of day, on specific days of the week, or at regular intervals.

Run the task: Once the task has been scheduled, analysts can run the script to start the automated process of collecting and analyzing data. The script will run in the background according to the specified schedule, ensuring that intelligence gathering efforts are consistently maintained and updated.

By scheduling and running automated tasks in OSINT using Python, analysts can save time and resources while ensuring a more consistent and thorough approach to intelligence gathering. Automation allows for the efficient collection and analysis of data from various online sources, enabling analysts to make informed decisions and support investigations with timely and relevant information. Python's simplicity and versatility make it an ideal tool for automating OSINT tasks, providing analysts with the ability to gather intelligence more effectively and efficiently.

Continuous Monitoring Techniques

Continuous monitoring techniques in language refer to the ongoing process of assessing and analyzing language skills, proficiency, and development over time. These techniques are used to track progress, identify areas for improvement, and make informed decisions about language learning and instruction. Continuous monitoring is essential for language learners of all levels, from beginners to advanced speakers, as it provides valuable insights into their language abilities and helps them achieve their language learning goals.

One of the key benefits of continuous monitoring techniques in language is that they allow for real-time feedback and assessment. By regularly assessing language skills and performance, teachers and learners can quickly identify areas of strength and weakness, and make adjustments to their learning strategies accordingly. This ongoing feedback loop helps to ensure that learners are progressing effectively and are able to address any challenges they may encounter in their language learning journey.

Continuous monitoring techniques in language also help to track progress and measure achievement over time. By regularly assessing language skills and proficiency levels, teachers and learners can see how far they have come and set goals for future improvement. This ongoing assessment process provides motivation and encouragement for learners, as they can see tangible evidence of their progress and success.

Another benefit of continuous monitoring techniques in language is that they allow for personalized and targeted instruction. By regularly assessing language skills and performance, teachers can tailor their instruction to meet the specific needs of individual learners. This personalized approach helps to ensure that learners are receiving the support and guidance they need to succeed in their language learning goals.

Continuous monitoring techniques in language also help to identify areas for improvement and areas of strength. By regularly assessing language skills and performance, teachers and learners can pinpoint specific areas that may need additional practice or attention. This targeted approach to language learning helps to focus efforts on areas that will have the greatest impact on overall language proficiency.

There are a variety of techniques that can be used for continuous monitoring in language learning. One common technique is the use of regular assessments, such as quizzes, tests, and exams, to measure language skills and proficiency levels. These assessments can be used to track progress over time and identify areas for improvement.

Another technique for continuous monitoring in language learning is the use of language portfolios. Language portfolios are collections of work samples, projects, and assessments that showcase a learner's language skills and achievements. By regularly updating and reviewing language portfolios, teachers and learners can track progress and measure achievement in a more holistic and comprehensive way.

Technology can also play a key role in continuous monitoring techniques in language learning. Online platforms and tools can be used to track progress, assess language skills, and provide feedback in real time. These digital resources can help to streamline the monitoring process and make it more efficient and effective for teachers and learners.

In conclusion, continuous monitoring techniques in language learning are essential for tracking progress, measuring achievement, and identifying areas for improvement. By regularly assessing language skills and proficiency levels, teachers and learners can make informed decisions about language learning and instruction.

These techniques help to personalize instruction, target areas for improvement, and provide motivation and encouragement for learners. By incorporating continuous monitoring techniques into language learning programs, educators can help learners achieve their language learning goals and succeed in their language learning journey.

Advanced Data Parsing Techniques

Data parsing is the process of extracting relevant information from a given dataset. In the field of language processing, advanced data parsing techniques are used to analyze and interpret textual data in a more sophisticated manner. These techniques involve the use of various algorithms and tools to extract meaningful insights from unstructured text data. In this article, we will explore some of the advanced data parsing techniques that are commonly used in language processing.

One of the most common advanced data parsing techniques used in language processing is natural language processing (NLP). NLP is a branch of artificial intelligence that focuses on the interaction between computers and humans using natural language. NLP techniques are used to analyze and understand the meaning of textual data, enabling computers to process and interpret human language. Some of the key NLP techniques used in data parsing include sentiment analysis, named entity recognition, and text summarization.

Sentiment analysis is a technique used to determine the sentiment or emotion expressed in a piece of text. This technique is commonly used in social media monitoring, customer feedback analysis, and opinion mining.
Sentiment analysis algorithms analyze the text to determine whether the sentiment expressed is positive, negative, or neutral. This information can be used to gauge public opinion, assess customer satisfaction, and make

informed business decisions.

Named entity recognition is another important NLP technique used in data parsing. Named entities are specific words or phrases that refer to real-world entities such as people, organizations, locations, dates, and numerical values. Named entity recognition algorithms are used to identify and classify named entities in a text document. This information can be used to extract relevant information, such as key players in a news article, important dates in a historical document, or financial figures in a business report.

Text summarization is a technique used to condense a large amount of text into a concise summary. Text summarization algorithms analyze the content of a text document and extract the most important information to create a summary. This technique is commonly used in news aggregation websites, search engines, and document summarization tools. Text summarization can help users quickly grasp the main points of a text document without having to read the entire content.

Another advanced data parsing technique used in language processing is part-of-speech tagging. Part-of-speech tagging is a technique used to assign grammatical categories (such as nouns, verbs, adjectives, etc.) to words in a text document. Part-of-speech tagging algorithms analyze the structure of a sentence to determine the grammatical role of each word. This information can be used to identify relationships between words, extract key phrases, and improve the accuracy of other NLP techniques.

In addition to these techniques, advanced data parsing in language processing also involves the use of machine learning algorithms such as deep learning and neural networks. These algorithms are used to train models that can automatically extract and analyze information from text data.

Deep learning algorithms, such as recurrent neural networks (RNNs) and convolutional neural networks (CNNs), are particularly effective at processing sequential data, such as text documents. These algorithms can learn complex patterns in the data and make accurate predictions based on the input.

Overall, advanced data parsing techniques in language processing play a crucial role in extracting meaningful insights from unstructured text data. By using a combination of NLP techniques, machine learning algorithms, and tools, researchers and practitioners can analyze and interpret textual data in a more sophisticated manner.

These techniques enable computers to understand human language, extract key information, and make informed decisions based on the data. As the field of language processing continues to evolve, advanced data parsing techniques will play an increasingly important role in unlocking the potential of textual data.

Chapter 16: Data Analysis and Visualization – OSINT

Data analysis and visualization in the field of Open Source Intelligence (OSINT) is a powerful tool that allows analysts to uncover valuable insights from a wide range of sources. By collecting and analyzing publicly available data, OSINT analysts can gain a deeper understanding of various topics, such as social media trends, geopolitical events, and cybersecurity threats.

One of the key benefits of using data analysis and visualization in OSINT is the ability to identify patterns and trends that may not be immediately apparent. By aggregating and analyzing data from multiple sources, analysts can uncover hidden connections and correlations that can help them make more informed decisions.

For example, social media platforms like Twitter and Facebook are rich sources of data that can be used to track public sentiment, identify key influencers, and monitor emerging trends. By analyzing the content of social media posts, OSINT analysts can gain insights into public opinion on a particular topic, detect potential threats, and even predict future events.

In addition to social media data, OSINT analysts can also leverage data from other sources, such as news articles, government reports, and public records. By collecting and analyzing data from a variety of sources, analysts can build a more comprehensive picture of a particular issue or event.

Data visualization plays a crucial role in OSINT analysis by helping analysts communicate their findings in a clear and concise manner. By using charts, graphs, and other visualizations, analysts can present complex data in a way that is easy to understand and interpret.

For example, a bar chart showing the number of social media posts mentioning a particular keyword over time can help analysts track the popularity of a specific topic. A network diagram showing the connections between different individuals or organizations can help analysts identify key players in a particular network.

In addition to helping analysts communicate their findings, data visualization can also help them identify new patterns and trends that may not be immediately apparent. By visualizing data in different ways, analysts can uncover insights that may have been overlooked in a traditional analysis.

There are a wide range of tools available for data analysis and visualization in OSINT, ranging from simple spreadsheet software to more advanced data mining and visualization platforms. Some popular tools used by OSINT analysts include Tableau, Palantir, and Maltego.

In conclusion, data analysis and visualization are powerful tools that can help OSINT analysts uncover valuable insights from a wide range of sources. By collecting and analyzing data from social media, news articles, and other sources, analysts can gain a deeper understanding of various topics and make more informed decisions. Data visualization plays a crucial role in helping analysts communicate their findings and identify new patterns and trends. Overall, data analysis and visualization are essential skills for any OSINT analyst looking to stay ahead in an increasingly complex and interconnected world.

Data Analysis with Pandas – Osint

Data analysis is an essential part of any business or organization, as it helps in making informed decisions based on data-driven insights. Pandas is a popular Python library that is widely used for data analysis and manipulation. In this article, we will explore how Pandas can be used for Open Source Intelligence (OSINT) data analysis.

OSINT refers to the collection and analysis of publicly available data from various sources such as social media, websites, and other online platforms. By analyzing this data, organizations can gather valuable information about their competitors, customers, and market trends.

Pandas provides a powerful set of tools for data manipulation, cleaning, and analysis, making it an ideal choice for OSINT data analysis. Let's take a look at some of the key features of Pandas that make it well-suited for this task:

Data Structures: Pandas provides two main data structures - Series and DataFrame. A Series is a one-dimensional array that can hold any data type, while a DataFrame is a two-dimensional table with rows and

204

columns. These data structures make it easy to work with structured data and perform various operations on it.

Data Cleaning: Before analyzing any data, it is important to clean and preprocess it to ensure its accuracy and consistency. Pandas provides functions for handling missing values, removing duplicates, and transforming data types, making it easy to clean and prepare data for analysis.

Data Manipulation: Pandas offers a wide range of functions for manipulating data, such as filtering rows, selecting columns, and grouping data based on certain criteria. These functions make it easy to extract relevant information from large datasets and perform complex analyses.

Data Visualization: Pandas integrates with other libraries like Matplotlib and Seaborn to create visualizations of data. Visualizations such as histograms, scatter plots, and bar charts can help in understanding patterns and trends in the data and communicating insights effectively.

Now, let's walk through a simple example of how Pandas can be used for OSINT data analysis. Suppose we have a dataset containing information about social media posts related to a particular topic. We want to analyze the sentiment of these posts and identify the most commonly used keywords.

First, we would import the necessary libraries:

```python
```

```python
import pandas as pd
import matplotlib.pyplot as plt import seaborn as sns
```

Next, we would load the dataset into a Pandas DataFrame:

```python
data = pd.read_csv('social_media_posts.csv')
```

We can then perform some basic data cleaning and preprocessing:

```python
# Remove duplicates
data = data.drop_duplicates()

# Handle missing values data = data.dropna()

# Convert text to lowercase data['text'] = data['text'].str.lower()
```

Next, we can analyze the sentiment of the posts using a sentiment analysis library like TextBlob:

```python
from textblob import TextBlob

# Function to calculate sentiment def get_sentiment(text):
analysis = TextBlob(text)
return analysis.sentiment.polarity
```

```python
# Apply sentiment analysis to each post data['sentiment']
= data['text'].apply(get_sentiment)
```

Finally, we can visualize the sentiment distribution and identify the most commonly used keywords:

```python
# Plot sentiment distribution
sns.histplot(data['sentiment'], bins=10)
plt.title('Sentiment Distribution of Social Media Posts')
plt.show()

# Identify keywords
keywords = data['text'].str.split(expand=True).stack().value_counts().head(10) print(keywords)
```

In this example, we have demonstrated how Pandas can be used for analyzing social media posts to extract sentiment and identify keywords. By leveraging the powerful features of Pandas, we can gain valuable insights from OSINT data and make informed decisions based on data-driven analysis.

In conclusion, Pandas is a versatile and powerful tool for data analysis, including OSINT data analysis. By using Pandas in conjunction with other libraries and tools, organizations can extract valuable insights from publicly

available data and make informed decisions based on data-driven analysis. Whether you are analyzing social media posts, website data, or any other type of publicly available data, Pandas can help you clean, manipulate, and analyze the data effectively.

Visualizing Data with Matplotlib – OSINT

Visualizing data is an essential part of any data analysis process. It helps to make sense of the information and communicate findings effectively. Matplotlib is a powerful data visualization library in Python that allows users to create a wide range of plots and charts. In this article, we will explore how to use Matplotlib for visualizing data in the context of OSINT (Open Source Intelligence).

OSINT is a method of collecting and analyzing data from publicly available sources to gather intelligence. It can be used for various purposes, such as cybersecurity, law enforcement, and business intelligence. Visualizing OSINT data can help analysts identify patterns, trends, and relationships in the data that may not be apparent from raw data alone.

To get started with visualizing data with Matplotlib in OSINT, you first need to install the library. You can do this by running the following command in your Python environment:

```
```

pip install matplotlib
```
```

Once Matplotlib is installed, you can start creating plots

and charts. The most common types of plots used in data visualization are line plots, bar plots, scatter plots, and histograms. Let's go through each of these and see how they can be used in the context of OSINT.

Line plots are used to show trends over time or to compare different datasets. For example, you can use a line plot to visualize the number of cyber attacks reported each month over a year. To create a line plot in Matplotlib, you can use the following code snippet:

```python
import matplotlib.pyplot as plt

# Data
months = ['Jan', 'Feb', 'Mar', 'Apr', 'May', 'Jun'] attacks = [100, 120, 90, 110, 130, 140]

# Create a line plot plt.plot(months, attacks) plt.xlabel('Month') plt.ylabel('Number of Attacks') plt.title('Cyber Attacks per Month') plt.show()
```

Bar plots are used to compare different categories or groups. For example, you can use a bar plot to visualize the number of attacks reported by different industries. To create a bar plot in Matplotlib, you can use the following code snippet:

```python

import matplotlib.pyplot as plt
```

```
# Data
industries = ['Finance', 'Healthcare', 'Government',
'Retail'] attacks = [200, 150, 100, 120]

# Create a bar plot plt.bar(industries, attacks)
plt.xlabel('Industry') plt.ylabel('Number of Attacks')
plt.title('Cyber Attacks by Industry') plt.show()
```

Scatter plots are used to show the relationship between two variables. For example, you can use a scatter plot to visualize the correlation between the number of social media mentions and the stock price of a company. To create a scatter plot in Matplotlib, you can use the following code snippet:

```python
import matplotlib.pyplot as plt

# Data
mentions = [10, 20, 30, 40, 50]
stock_price = [100, 120, 130, 140, 150]

# Create a scatter plot plt.scatter(mentions, stock_price)
plt.xlabel('Social Media Mentions') plt.ylabel('Stock Price')
plt.title('Correlation between Social Media Mentions and
Stock Price') plt.show()
```

Histograms are used to visualize the distribution of a single variable. For example, you can use a histogram to visualize the distribution of the number of data breaches reported in a year. To create a histogram in Matplotlib, you can use the following code snippet:

```python
import matplotlib.pyplot as plt

# Data
data_breaches = [50, 60, 70, 80, 90, 100, 110, 120, 130, 140]

# Create a histogram plt.hist(data_breaches, bins=5)
plt.xlabel('Number of Data Breaches')
plt.ylabel('Frequency')

plt.title('Distribution of Data Breaches') plt.show()
```

In addition to these basic plots, Matplotlib also provides support for creating more advanced plots, such as pie charts, box plots, and heatmaps. These plots can be useful for visualizing different aspects of OSINT data, such as the distribution of threats by country or the frequency of keywords in social media posts.

Overall, Matplotlib is a versatile and powerful library for visualizing data in the context of OSINT. By using different types of plots and charts, analysts can gain valuable insights from the data and communicate their findings effectively. Whether you are analyzing cybersecurity threats, monitoring social media activity, or conducting competitive intelligence, Matplotlib can help you create informative and visually appealing visualizations.

Creating Interactive Dashboards – Osint

Creating interactive dashboards for Open Source Intelligence (OSINT) is a powerful way to visualize and analyze data from various sources to gain valuable insights. OSINT is a valuable tool for gathering information from publicly available sources such as social media, news articles, and websites to gather intelligence on a particular subject or target. By creating interactive dashboards, analysts can quickly and easily sift through large amounts of data to identify patterns, trends, and anomalies.

To create interactive dashboards for OSINT, analysts can use a variety of tools and techniques to collect, clean, and analyze data. One popular tool for creating interactive dashboards is Tableau, a data visualization software that allows users to create interactive and dynamic visualizations of their data. Tableau allows users to connect to various data sources, including spreadsheets, databases, and web services, to create visually appealing dashboards that can be shared and accessed by others.

To create an interactive dashboard in Tableau for OSINT, analysts can start by defining their objectives and identifying the key data sources they want to analyze. For example, if an analyst is interested in monitoring social media activity related to a particular topic, they can connect to Twitter or Facebook APIs to gather data on posts, likes, shares, and comments related to that topic.

Once the data sources have been connected, analysts can begin to clean and transform the data to make it suitable for analysis. This may involve removing duplicates, fixing missing values, and aggregating data to create meaningful metrics. Analysts can then use Tableau's drag-and-drop interface to create visualizations such as bar charts, line graphs, and heat maps to identify patterns and trends in the data.

To make the dashboard interactive, analysts can add filters, parameters, and actions to allow users to explore the data in more detail. For example, analysts can add a filter that allows users to select a specific date range or keyword to focus on a particular subset of the data. They can also add actions that link different visualizations together so that clicking on a data point in one chart updates the data in another chart.

In addition to Tableau, analysts can also use other tools such as Power BI, Google Data Studio, and D3.js to create interactive dashboards for OSINT. Each tool has its strengths and weaknesses, so analysts should choose the tool that best fits their needs and skill level.

In conclusion, creating interactive dashboards for OSINT is a valuable skill for analysts looking to gain insights from large amounts of data. By using tools such as Tableau, analysts can connect to various data sources, clean and transform the data, and create visually appealing visualizations that allow users to explore the data in more detail. With the right tools and techniques, analysts can uncover valuable insights that can inform decision-making and drive strategic outcomes.

Chapter 17: OSINT with Shodan

Open Source Intelligence (OSINT) is a crucial aspect of modern intelligence gathering, allowing organizations and individuals to gather information from publicly available sources. One powerful tool that is often used in OSINT operations is Shodan, a search engine that allows users to find information about internet-connected devices.

Shodan is unique in that it focuses on gathering data about the devices themselves, rather than the content that they host. This can include information such as the type of device, its location, and even details about its security settings. By using Shodan, OSINT analysts can gain valuable insights into the security posture of organizations, identify potential vulnerabilities, and even track down specific devices or networks.

One of the key benefits of using Shodan in OSINT operations is its ability to provide real-time data. Unlike traditional search engines that index web pages, Shodan scans the internet for specific types of devices, such as webcams, routers, and servers. This means that users can access up-to-date information about the devices that are connected to the internet, allowing them to quickly identify potential threats or vulnerabilities.

Another advantage of using Shodan in OSINT operations is its ease of use. The search engine is designed to be user-friendly, with a simple interface that allows users to enter search queries and quickly access relevant information. This makes it an ideal tool for both experienced analysts and those who are new to OSINT operations.

In addition to its ease of use, Shodan also offers a range of advanced search capabilities that can help users to refine their queries and find specific information. For example, users can search for devices based on their location, IP address, or even specific keywords that are contained within the device's metadata. This level of granularity can be invaluable in OSINT operations, allowing analysts to quickly identify relevant information and make informed decisions.

One of the key use cases for Shodan in OSINT operations is identifying vulnerable devices that are connected to the internet. By searching for specific types of devices, such as unsecured webcams or routers with default passwords, analysts can quickly identify potential targets for cyber attacks. This can help organizations to proactively secure their networks and prevent data breaches before they occur.

Shodan can also be used to track down specific devices or networks that are of interest to OSINT analysts. For example, researchers investigating a particular threat actor may use Shodan to identify all of the devices that are associated with that actor, allowing them to build a comprehensive picture of their activities. This type of targeted searching can be invaluable in OSINT operations, allowing analysts to quickly gather relevant information and make connections between different pieces of data.

Overall, Shodan is a powerful tool that can provide valuable insights for OSINT operations. By using the search engine to gather information about internet-connected devices, analysts can identify potential threats, track down specific targets, and make informed decisions about cybersecurity. With its real-time data, user-friendly interface, and advanced search capabilities, Shodan is an essential tool for anyone involved in OSINT operations.

Advanced Techniques with Shodan and Python

Shodan is a powerful search engine that allows users to find specific types of computers, devices, and services connected to the internet. It is often used by security researchers, penetration testers, and hackers to discover vulnerable systems and services. In this article, we will explore advanced searching techniques with Shodan using Python.

Getting Started
To use Shodan with Python, you will need to install the Shodan library. You can do this by running the following command:

```
```

```
pip install shodan
```

After installing the library, you will need to create a Shodan account and obtain an API key. You can sign up for a free account on the Shodan website and generate an API key from your account settings.

Searching with Shodan
Shodan allows users to perform advanced searches using

various filters and operators. Some of the common filters include country, hostname, port, operating system, and organization. You can combine multiple filters to narrow down your search results.

Here is an example of a basic search query using the Shodan API:

```python
import shodan

api_key = 'YOUR_API_KEY'
query = 'apache'
api = shodan.Shodan(api_key)
results = api.search(query)
for result in results['matches']:
    print(result['ip_str'])
```

In this example, we are searching for devices that have "apache" in their banners. The search results will include the IP addresses of the matching devices.

Advanced Searching Techniques
To perform more advanced searches with Shodan, you can use the following techniques:

Filtering by Port
You can filter search results by specific ports using the "port" filter. For example, to find devices running on port 80, you can use the following query:

```python
query = 'port:80'
```

Filtering by Country
You can filter search results by country using the "country" filter. For example, to find devices in the United States, you can use the following query:

```python
query = 'country:US'
```

Filtering by Operating System
You can filter search results by operating system using the "os" filter. For example, to find devices running on Windows, you can use the following query:

```python
query = 'os:windows'
```

Combining Filters
You can combine multiple filters to perform more specific searches. For example, to find devices in the United States running on port 80, you can use the following query:

```python
```

```python
query = 'country:US port:80'
```

Searching for Vulnerabilities

You can search for specific vulnerabilities using the "vuln" filter. For example, to find devices vulnerable to the Heartbleed bug, you can use the following query:

```python
query = 'vuln:heartbleed'
```

Searching for Webcams

You can search for webcams using the "webcam" filter. For example, to find webcams in the United States, you can use the following query:

```python
query = 'country:US webcam'
```

Searching for Industrial Control Systems

You can search for industrial control systems using the "ics" filter. For example, to find devices in the United States that are part of an industrial control system, you can use the following query:

```python
query = 'country:US ics'
```

Searching for Specific Services

You can search for specific services using the "product"

filter. For example, to find devices running on the Apache web server, you can use the following query:

```python
query = 'product:apache'
```

Conclusion
In this article, we have explored advanced searching techniques with Shodan using Python. By combining various filters and operators, you can perform specific searches to find vulnerable devices, webcams, industrial control systems, and more. Shodan is a powerful tool that can be used for security research, penetration testing, and reconnaissance. Experiment with different search queries to discover interesting devices and services connected to the internet.

Analyzing Shodan Data

Shodan is a search engine that allows users to find and analyze internet-connected devices. It is often used by security professionals to identify vulnerabilities in their networks and systems. By analyzing Shodan data, users can gain valuable insights into the state of their network security and take appropriate actions to protect their systems from potential threats.

One of the key features of Shodan is its ability to scan the internet for open ports and services. By analyzing the data collected by Shodan, users can identify which ports and services are open on their network and determine if any of them are vulnerable to attack. For example, if Shodan detects that a device on the network has an open port that is commonly targeted by hackers, users can take steps to secure that port and prevent unauthorized access.

Another valuable aspect of analyzing Shodan data is the ability to identify devices that are connected to the internet but may not be properly secured. For example, Shodan can detect devices such as webcams, routers, and printers that are accessible from the internet without proper authentication. By analyzing this data, users can identify potential security risks and take steps to secure these devices to prevent unauthorized access.

In addition to identifying vulnerabilities in network devices, analyzing Shodan data can also help users track the spread of malware and other malicious software. By monitoring the internet-connected devices that are hosting malware, users can gain insights into how these threats are spreading and take action to protect their own systems from infection. For example, if Shodan detects that a particular IP address is hosting malware, users can block that IP address from accessing their network to prevent the spread of the malware.

Furthermore, analyzing Shodan data can also help users identify trends in internet-connected devices and services. By analyzing the types of devices that are connected to the internet and the services they are running, users can gain insights into how technology is evolving and adapt their security strategies accordingly. For example, if Shodan detects a rise in the number of internet-connected devices running outdated software, users can take steps to update their own systems and prevent potential security vulnerabilities.

Overall, analyzing Shodan data can provide valuable insights into the state of network security and help users identify potential vulnerabilities in their systems. By monitoring internet-connected devices, tracking the spread of malware, and identifying trends in technology, users can take proactive steps to protect their networks and systems from potential threats. In an increasingly connected world, analyzing Shodan data is an essential tool for maintaining network security and protecting against cyber threats.

Chapter 18: Machine Learning for OSINT

Machine learning is a branch of artificial intelligence that involves the development of algorithms and models that enable computers to learn from and make predictions or decisions based on data. In recent years, machine learning has become increasingly important in the field of open-source intelligence (OSINT), which involves collecting and analyzing information from publicly available sources such as social media, news articles, and government reports.

Machine learning algorithms can be used to automate the process of collecting and analyzing large volumes of OSINT data, making it easier for analysts to identify patterns, trends, and relationships that may not be immediately apparent to the human eye. By training machine learning models on historical data, analysts can develop predictive models that can help anticipate future events or identify potential threats.

One of the key advantages of using machine learning for OSINT is its ability to process and analyze vast amounts of data quickly and efficiently. Traditional methods of collecting and analyzing OSINT data, such as manual searches or keyword-based queries, can be time-consuming and labor-intensive. Machine learning algorithms, on the other hand, can sift through large volumes of data in a fraction of the time it would take a human analyst, allowing for faster and more accurate insights.

Machine learning can also help analysts uncover hidden patterns or connections in OSINT data that may not be immediately obvious. For example, machine learning algorithms can be used to identify clusters of social media users who are discussing a particular topic or event, even if they do not explicitly mention it in their posts. By analyzing the language, tone, and sentiment of these posts, analysts can gain a better understanding of public opinion and sentiment surrounding a particular issue.

In addition to analyzing text data, machine learning algorithms can also be used to process and analyze images and videos from OSINT sources. For example, image recognition algorithms can be used to identify objects, people, or locations in photos and videos, helping analysts to piece together a more complete picture of a particular event or situation. Video analysis algorithms can also be used to detect patterns of movement or behavior in surveillance footage, helping analysts to track the movements of individuals or groups of interest.

Machine learning can also be used to automate the process of monitoring and analyzing OSINT data in real-time. By setting up automated data collection and analysis pipelines, analysts can receive alerts or notifications when certain keywords or topics of interest are mentioned in online sources. This can help analysts stay ahead of emerging threats or trends and respond more quickly to developing situations.

Despite its many advantages, using machine learning for OSINT also comes with its own set of challenges and limitations. For example, machine learning algorithms are only as good as the data they are trained on, and biases or inaccuracies in the training data can lead to biased or inaccurate predictions. Additionally, machine learning algorithms can struggle with noisy or unstructured data, such as social media posts or news articles that contain slang, sarcasm, or misinformation.

In conclusion, machine learning has the potential to revolutionize the field of OSINT by enabling analysts to process and analyze vast amounts of data quickly and efficiently. By training machine learning models on historical data, analysts can develop predictive models that can help anticipate future events or identify potential threats. However, using machine learning for OSINT also comes with its own set of challenges and limitations, and analysts must be mindful of these when developing and deploying machine learning solutions in their intelligence workflows.

Ext Mining and Analysis – OSINT

Open Source Intelligence (OSINT) is a valuable tool for gathering information from publicly available sources. OSINT can be used for a variety of purposes, including market research, competitive analysis, threat intelligence, and more. One area where OSINT is particularly useful is in the field of external mining and analysis.

External mining and analysis refers to the process of collecting and analyzing information from external sources to gain insights into a particular topic, organization, or individual. This can include everything from social media

225

posts and news articles to website content and public records. By leveraging OSINT techniques, analysts can uncover valuable insights that may not be readily apparent through traditional research methods.

One key aspect of external mining and analysis is the ability to gather information from a wide range of sources. This can include social media platforms such as Twitter, Facebook, and LinkedIn, as well as news websites, blogs, forums, and more. By casting a wide net and collecting data from multiple sources, analysts can gain a comprehensive understanding of their target and identify potential trends or patterns.

In addition to collecting data from external sources, analysts must also be able to analyze and interpret the information they gather. This can involve identifying key themes or trends, assessing the credibility of sources, and drawing connections between different pieces of information. By applying advanced analytical techniques, analysts can extract valuable insights from the data they collect and use this information to inform decision-making processes.

One of the key benefits of external mining and analysis is the ability to monitor and track developments in real-time. By continuously monitoring external sources, analysts can stay up-to-date on the latest news, trends, and events related to their target. This can help organizations identify emerging threats, opportunities, or challenges and respond proactively to changing circumstances.

Another important aspect of external mining and analysis is the ability to identify and assess potential risks. By monitoring external sources for indicators of potential threats or vulnerabilities, analysts can help organizations mitigate risks and protect their assets. This can include monitoring social media for mentions of security breaches, tracking news articles for reports of cyber attacks, or analyzing public records for information on regulatory compliance.

In conclusion, external mining and analysis using OSINT techniques can provide organizations with valuable insights into their target environment. By collecting and analyzing information from external sources, analysts can gain a comprehensive understanding of their target, identify potential risks, and stay up-to-date on the latest developments. By leveraging OSINT tools and techniques, organizations can make informed decisions, mitigate risks, and stay ahead of the competition.

Predictive OSINT Analysis

Predictive Open Source Intelligence (OSINT) analysis is a rapidly evolving field that leverages publicly available information to anticipate and predict future events. By analyzing data from social media, news articles, blogs, and other online sources, analysts can identify patterns, trends, and potential threats before they materialize.

One of the key benefits of predictive OSINT analysis is its ability to provide early warning of emerging risks and opportunities. By monitoring online conversations and tracking the activities of individuals and organizations,

227

analysts can identify potential threats to national security, business operations, or public safety. For example, by analyzing social media posts and news articles, analysts can detect signs of political unrest, cyber threats, or terrorist activities before they escalate.

In addition to identifying potential risks, predictive OSINT analysis can also help organizations make informed decisions and develop effective strategies. By analyzing online data, analysts can gain insights into consumer behavior, market trends, and competitor activities. This information can be used to develop targeted marketing campaigns, improve product offerings, or identify new business opportunities.

One of the key challenges of predictive OSINT analysis is the sheer volume of data that analysts must sift through. With billions of social media posts, news articles, and online discussions published every day, analysts must use advanced analytics tools and techniques to filter out irrelevant information and identify relevant patterns and trends. This requires a combination of machine learning algorithms, natural language processing techniques, and human expertise to make sense of the data.

Another challenge of predictive OSINT analysis is the need to verify the accuracy and reliability of the information. Because much of the data used in OSINT analysis comes from publicly available sources, there is a risk of misinformation, disinformation, or manipulation. Analysts must carefully evaluate the credibility of the sources and cross-reference information from multiple sources to ensure its accuracy.

Despite these challenges, predictive OSINT analysis has proven to be a valuable tool for a wide range of industries and organizations. In the intelligence community, OSINT analysis is used to monitor threats to national security, track the activities of terrorist organizations, and identify potential sources of instability. In the business world, OSINT analysis is used to monitor competitor activities, track consumer sentiment, and identify emerging market trends.

As the field of predictive OSINT analysis continues to evolve, analysts are exploring new techniques and technologies to improve the accuracy and reliability of their predictions. For example, some analysts are using social network analysis to identify key influencers and opinion leaders who can provide valuable insights into emerging trends and events. Others are using sentiment analysis to gauge public sentiment and predict how individuals and groups are likely to react to certain events.

Overall, predictive OSINT analysis is a powerful tool that can help organizations anticipate and respond to emerging risks and opportunities. By leveraging publicly available information and advanced analytics techniques, analysts can gain valuable insights into future events and make informed decisions that can help mitigate risks and capitalize on opportunities. As the field continues to evolve, predictive OSINT analysis is likely to play an increasingly important role in shaping the future of intelligence and business operations.

Chapter 19: Understanding Counter-OSINT

Open Source Intelligence (OSINT) has become a critical tool for gathering information in today's digital age. It allows individuals and organizations to access publicly available information to gain insights, make informed decisions, and mitigate risks. However, as the use of OSINT has grown, so too has the need for counter-OSINT strategies to protect sensitive information and prevent adversaries from using open-source data against them.

In this chapter, we will explore the concept of counter-OSINT, its importance, and various strategies that can be employed to counter the use of OSINT against individuals and organizations.

Understanding Counter-OSINT

Counter-OSINT refers to the practice of identifying, analyzing, and mitigating threats posed by the use of OSINT by adversaries. This can include individuals, organizations, or even nation-states seeking to exploit publicly available information for malicious purposes. The goal of counter-OSINT is to protect sensitive information, maintain operational security, and prevent adversaries from gaining an advantage through the use of open-source data.

Counter-OSINT is a complex and evolving field that requires a deep understanding of OSINT techniques, tools, and sources. It involves a combination of technical expertise, analytical skills, and strategic thinking to effectively identify and neutralize threats posed by adversaries using OSINT.

Importance of Counter-OSINT

The importance of counter-OSINT cannot be overstated in today's interconnected world. As the volume and variety of open-source data continue to grow, so too do the risks associated with its use by adversaries. From social media posts to publicly available databases, there is a wealth of information that can be exploited for malicious purposes.

By understanding and implementing counter-OSINT strategies, individuals and organizations can protect themselves from a range of threats, including data breaches, social engineering attacks, and reputational damage. Counter-OSINT can help identify vulnerabilities in an organization's digital footprint, assess the effectiveness of existing security measures, and develop proactive strategies to mitigate risks.

Counter-OSINT Strategies

There are several strategies that can be employed to counter the use of OSINT by adversaries. These include:

Threat Intelligence: By monitoring and analyzing online threats, organizations can identify potential adversaries and their tactics. This information can be used to develop counter-OSINT strategies and enhance overall security posture.

Information Control: Organizations can limit the amount of sensitive information that is publicly available by implementing strict privacy settings on social media accounts, restricting access to sensitive data, and monitoring the release of sensitive information.

Deception: Counter-OSINT tactics can involve the use of deception to mislead adversaries and protect sensitive information. This can include the creation of fake personas, false information, and disinformation campaigns to confuse and deter adversaries.

Monitoring and Analysis: By continuously monitoring and analyzing open-source data, organizations can identify potential threats and vulnerabilities in real-time. This proactive approach can help prevent adversaries from exploiting vulnerabilities before they can cause harm.

Collaboration: Counter-OSINT is a collaborative effort that requires coordination between various stakeholders, including security professionals, intelligence analysts, and law enforcement agencies. By sharing information and resources, organizations can enhance their ability to counter threats posed by adversaries using OSINT.

Conclusion

Counter-OSINT is an essential component of modern cybersecurity and intelligence operations. By understanding the risks posed by the use of OSINT by adversaries and implementing effective counter-OSINT strategies, individuals and organizations can protect sensitive information, maintain operational security, and prevent adversaries from gaining an advantage through the use of open-source data.

Protecting Your Privacy – OSINT

In today's digital age, protecting your privacy has become more important than ever. With the rise of social media, online shopping, and digital communication, our personal information is constantly being collected and stored by various companies and organizations. This has led to an increase in the number of data breaches and privacy violations, making it crucial for individuals to take steps to protect their personal information.

One way to protect your privacy online is to use open-source intelligence (OSINT) tools such as Python. OSINT refers to the collection and analysis of publicly available information from various sources, including social media, websites, and online databases. By using Python, a versatile and powerful programming language, you can automate the process of gathering and analyzing data to better protect your privacy online.

In this article, we will discuss the importance of protecting your privacy, the role of OSINT in safeguarding your personal information, and how Python can be used to enhance your online privacy.

Why is Privacy Important?

Privacy is a fundamental human right that is essential for

maintaining autonomy, dignity, and freedom. In the digital age, our personal information is constantly being collected and shared by various entities, including social media platforms, online retailers, and government agencies. This has led to an erosion of privacy, with individuals often unaware of how their personal data is being used and shared.

Protecting your privacy is important for several reasons. First and foremost, it helps prevent identity theft, fraud, and other forms of cybercrime. By safeguarding your personal information, you can reduce the risk of falling victim to malicious actors who may use your data for nefarious purposes.

Second, protecting your privacy helps preserve your online reputation. In today's interconnected world, our digital footprint plays a significant role in shaping how others perceive us. By controlling the information that is available about you online, you can ensure that your online presence accurately reflects who you are.

Finally, protecting your privacy is essential for maintaining your personal autonomy. In an era where data is constantly being collected and analyzed, it is easy for individuals to feel like they are being watched or monitored. By taking steps to protect your privacy, you can reclaim control over your personal information and ensure that your digital identity remains private and secure.

The Role of OSINT in Protecting Your Privacy

Open-source intelligence (OSINT) refers to the collection

and analysis of publicly available information from various sources, including social media, websites, and online databases. OSINT tools are commonly used by law enforcement agencies, security professionals, and researchers to gather information about individuals, organizations, and events.

In the context of protecting your privacy, OSINT can be a valuable tool for monitoring and controlling the information that is available about you online. By using OSINT tools to gather data from social media platforms, websites, and other sources, you can gain insights into how your personal information is being shared and used by others.

For example, OSINT tools can be used to monitor your online presence and identify potential privacy risks. By analyzing the information that is publicly available about you, you can determine whether your personal data is being shared without your consent or used in ways that could compromise your privacy.

OSINT tools can also be used to conduct threat intelligence analysis, which involves identifying and mitigating potential security threats. By monitoring online forums, social media platforms, and other sources of information, you can identify potential threats to your privacy and take proactive steps to protect your personal information.

Overall, OSINT can be a powerful tool for safeguarding your privacy online. By using OSINT tools to gather and analyze publicly available information, you can gain insights into how your personal data is being used and shared, identify potential privacy risks, and take proactive steps to protect your privacy.

Using Python for OSINT

Python is a versatile and powerful programming language that is widely used in the field of cybersecurity and data analysis. With its simple syntax and extensive library of modules, Python is well-suited for developing OSINT tools that can automate the process of gathering and analyzing data from various sources.

There are several Python libraries and frameworks that can be used for OSINT, including:

Requests: A Python library for making HTTP requests, which can be used to retrieve data from websites and APIs.
BeautifulSoup: A Python library for parsing HTML and XML documents, which can be used to extract information from web pages.
Scrapy: A Python framework for web scraping, which can be used to automate the process of gathering data from websites.
Shodan: A Python library for interacting with the Shodan search engine, which can be used to gather information about internet-connected devices.

By using these and other Python libraries, you can develop custom OSINT tools that can automate the process of gathering and analyzing data from various online sources. These tools can be used to monitor your online presence, identify potential privacy risks, and take proactive steps to protect your personal information.

Analyzing and Reducing Your Digital Footprint

In today's digital age, it's more important than ever to be conscious of the information we put out into the world. With the rise of social media, online shopping, and other digital platforms, our digital footprint has become larger and more complex than ever before. This can have serious implications for our privacy and security, as well as our personal and professional reputations.

One way to take control of your digital footprint is through open-source intelligence (OSINT) techniques. OSINT refers to the practice of collecting and analyzing publicly available information to gather intelligence on a particular target. This can include information from social media, websites, forums, and other online sources.

One popular tool for conducting OSINT is Python, a versatile and powerful programming language that is widely used in the cybersecurity and data analysis fields. In this article, we'll explore how you can use Python to analyze and reduce your digital footprint, helping you protect your privacy and security online.

Analyzing Your Digital Footprint with Python

One of the first steps in reducing your digital footprint is to analyze the information that is already out there about you. This can help you identify potential security risks and areas where you may be inadvertently sharing too much personal information.

Python can be a valuable tool for this task, as it allows you to automate the process of collecting and analyzing data from various online sources. For example, you can use Python to scrape social media profiles, websites, and other online platforms for information about yourself. This can help you identify where your personal information is being shared and take steps to limit its exposure.

Python also offers powerful data analysis tools that can help you make sense of the information you collect. For example, you can use Python to analyze the frequency of certain keywords or phrases in your online profiles, helping you identify patterns in your online behavior. This can help you understand how much information you are sharing and where you may need to be more cautious.

Reducing Your Digital Footprint with Python

Once you have analyzed your digital footprint, the next step is to take action to reduce it. This can involve deleting or limiting the information you share online, as well as taking steps to protect your privacy and security.

Python can be a valuable tool for this task as well. For example, you can use Python to automate the process of deleting old social media posts or accounts. This can help you clean up your online presence and reduce the amount of personal information that is available about you.

Python can also be used to enhance your online security. For example, you can use Python to automate the process of changing your passwords regularly or setting up two-factor authentication on your accounts. This can help protect your accounts from unauthorized access and reduce the risk of identity theft.

In addition to these technical measures, there are also steps you can take in your everyday online behavior to reduce your digital footprint. For example, you can be more cautious about the information you share online, avoiding posting sensitive personal information or location data. You can also be mindful of the privacy settings on your social media accounts, limiting who can see your posts and information.

By combining these technical and behavioral measures, you can take control of your digital footprint and reduce the risk to your privacy and security online.

Analyzing and reducing your digital footprint is an important step in protecting your privacy and security online. By using OSINT techniques and Python, you can automate the process of collecting and analyzing information about yourself, helping you identify potential security risks and areas where you may be sharing too much personal information.

Python also offers powerful tools for reducing your digital footprint, allowing you to automate the process of deleting old social media posts, changing passwords, and enhancing your online security. By combining these technical measures with mindful online behavior, you can take control of your digital footprint and reduce the risk to your privacy and security online.

Overall, taking steps to analyze and reduce your digital footprint is an important part of being a responsible and secure internet user. By being conscious of the information you put out into the world and taking steps to protect your privacy and security, you can enjoy the benefits of the digital age without compromising your personal information.

Anonymity strategies for OSINT - using advanced techniques in Python

Anonymity is a critical aspect of conducting open-source intelligence (OSINT) investigations, as it allows researchers to gather information without revealing their identities. In this article, we will explore advanced techniques in Python that can be used to enhance anonymity while conducting OSINT investigations.

One of the most common ways to maintain anonymity in OSINT investigations is by using proxies. Proxies act as intermediaries between the user and the target website, masking the user's IP address and location. There are many free and paid proxy services available, but it is important to choose a reliable and secure service to ensure anonymity.

Python has several libraries that can be used to work with proxies, such as requests and urllib. These libraries allow users to specify a proxy server when making HTTP requests, effectively hiding their IP address. By rotating between multiple proxies, users can further enhance their anonymity and avoid detection by websites that may block suspicious IP addresses.

240

Another advanced technique for maintaining anonymity in OSINT investigations is by using Tor. Tor is a free and open-source software that allows users to browse the internet anonymously by routing their traffic through a series of encrypted relays. By using Tor, users can hide their IP address and location, making it difficult for websites to track their activities.

Python has a library called stem that can be used to interact with the Tor network. By configuring stem to route traffic through the Tor network, users can conduct OSINT investigations anonymously and avoid detection. It is important to note that using Tor may slow down internet speeds, so users should be prepared for potential delays when conducting research.

In addition to proxies and Tor, users can also enhance their anonymity by using virtual private networks (VPNs). VPNs encrypt internet traffic and route it through a secure server, effectively hiding the user's IP address and location. There are many VPN services available, both free and paid, that can be used to maintain anonymity while conducting OSINT investigations.

Python has libraries that can be used to work with VPNs, such as openvpn and nordvpn. By configuring these libraries to connect to a VPN server, users can ensure that their internet traffic is encrypted and secure. VPNs are particularly useful for users who need to access geographically restricted websites or services while maintaining anonymity.

Another advanced technique for enhancing anonymity in OSINT investigations is by using disposable email addresses. Disposable email addresses are temporary email accounts that can be used to sign up for websites or services without revealing the user's real email address. By using disposable email addresses, users can protect their identities and avoid spam or unwanted emails.

Python has libraries that can be used to create disposable email addresses, such as tempmail and temp-mail. By generating a temporary email address with these libraries, users can sign up for websites or services anonymously and receive emails without revealing their real email address. This can be particularly useful for users who need to create multiple accounts for research purposes.

In addition to proxies, Tor, VPNs, and disposable email addresses, users can also enhance their anonymity by using virtual machines. Virtual machines are isolated environments that can be used to run applications or browse the internet without affecting the user's main operating system. By using a virtual machine, users can create a clean and secure environment for conducting OSINT investigations.

Python has libraries that can be used to interact with virtual machines, such as virtualenv and vagrant. By configuring these libraries to create a virtual machine, users can ensure that their activities are isolated from their main operating system and maintain anonymity while conducting research. Virtual machines are particularly useful for users who need to test potentially malicious websites or applications without risking their main system.

In conclusion, maintaining anonymity is crucial when conducting OSINT investigations, as it allows researchers to gather information without revealing their identities. By using advanced techniques in Python, such as proxies, Tor, VPNs, disposable email addresses, and virtual machines, users can enhance their anonymity and avoid detection by websites or services. It is important to choose reliable and secure services when implementing these techniques to ensure that anonymity is maintained throughout the investigation. By following best practices and using the right tools, users can conduct OSINT investigations safely and effectively.

Conclusion

In conclusion, the future of Python in OSINT looks incredibly promising. As one of the most popular programming languages in the world, Python has already made a significant impact on the field of open source intelligence, and its influence is only expected to grow in the coming years.

One of the key reasons for Python's success in OSINT is its versatility and ease of use. Python's simple and readable syntax makes it an ideal choice for beginners and experienced programmers alike. Its extensive library of modules and packages also allows users to quickly and easily access and manipulate data from a wide range of sources, making it a powerful tool for conducting open source intelligence gathering.

Furthermore, Python's strong community support and active development ecosystem ensure that the language will continue to evolve and adapt to the changing needs of OSINT practitioners. This means that Python will remain a relevant and valuable tool for conducting open source intelligence operations well into the future.

Another factor contributing to Python's success in OSINT is its compatibility with a wide range of operating systems and platforms. Whether you are using Windows, macOS, or Linux, Python can be easily installed and run on your system, making it accessible to a broad audience of users.

Additionally, Python's integration with other programming languages and tools further enhances its capabilities in OSINT. For example, Python can be easily combined with web scraping tools like Beautiful Soup or data visualization libraries like Matplotlib to create powerful and sophisticated intelligence gathering and analysis workflows.

Looking ahead, the future of Python in OSINT will likely be shaped by advancements in artificial intelligence and machine learning. As these technologies become more prevalent in the field of intelligence gathering, Python's ability to easily integrate with AI and ML frameworks will make it an indispensable tool for OSINT practitioners.

Furthermore, as the volume and complexity of data continue to increase, Python's ability to handle large datasets and perform complex data analysis will be crucial for conducting effective open source intelligence operations. With its robust data processing capabilities and extensive library of data manipulation tools, Python is well- positioned to meet the growing demands of the OSINT community.

In conclusion, Python's future in OSINT is bright. Its versatility, ease of use, compatibility with other tools, and integration with emerging technologies make it a powerful and indispensable tool for conducting open source intelligence operations. As the field of OSINT continues to evolve, Python will undoubtedly play a key role in shaping the future of intelligence gathering and analysis. With its strong community support and active development ecosystem, Python is well-positioned to remain at the forefront of OSINT for years to come.

Biography

Jason Bourny is a seasoned cybersecurity expert, hacker, and passionate advocate for the power of open-source intelligence (OSINT). With over a decade of experience in the field, Jason has honed his skills in penetration testing, ethical hacking, and advanced data extraction methods, making him a sought-after authority in the world of digital security.

Jason's journey began with a fascination for coding and a love for the intricacies of Python. This passion quickly evolved into a full-fledged career as he delved deeper into the realms of OSINT and cybersecurity. His expertise in Python for web scraping and data extraction has not only made him a master in his field but also a mentor to many aspiring hackers and cybersecurity professionals.

When he's not diving into code or unraveling the complexities of the digital world, Jason enjoys exploring the latest technological advancements and staying ahead of the curve in cybersecurity trends. He is an avid contributor to online forums and communities, where he shares his knowledge and collaborates with fellow enthusiasts to push the boundaries of what's possible in OSINT.

In addition to his professional pursuits, Jason is an adrenaline junkie who loves outdoor adventures and tackling new challenges. Whether it's hiking through rugged terrains or participating in hackathons, his enthusiasm for learning and exploration knows no bounds.

With "Python for OSINT: Tracking and Profiling Targets," Jason brings his wealth of knowledge and infectious enthusiasm to help readers master advanced web scraping and data extraction techniques. His engaging teaching style and practical insights make this ebook a must-read for anyone looking to elevate their skills in the ever-evolving landscape of cybersecurity and OSINT.

Join Jason Bourny on this exciting journey and unlock the full potential of Python for your OSINT endeavors. Get ready to dive deep, learn immensely, and transform the way you approach data extraction and intelligence gathering!